INDESCRIBABLE
ACTIVITY BOOK
FOR KIDS

150+ MIND-STRETCHING AND
FAITH-BUILDING PUZZLES, CROSSWORDS,
STEM EXPERIMENTS, AND MORE
ABOUT GOD AND SCIENCE!

LOUIE GIGLIO

WITH TAMA FORTNER

ILLUSTRATED BY NICOLA ANDERSON
& LYNSEY WILSON

Tommy
NELSON
An Imprint of Thomas Nelson

passionpublishing

T0063837

MEET THE INDESCRIBABLE KIDS!

The Indescribable gang loves adventuring, exploring, and discovering. Most of all, they love getting to know the God who created them and this wildly wonderful world!

RAZ

Raz is usually busy skateboarding, building, or chowing down on pizza. One day he hopes to travel the world and explore all the different ecosystems, from deserts to rainforests.

EVYN

Evyn loves basketball and is a whiz at reading. She never turns down a taco and would spend every day at the beach if she could.

NORAH

Norah loves her dog, Penny, even more than her favorite dessert—ice cream! When she's not playing soccer or drawing, you'll find her out in nature exploring God's amazing creations.

JOSHUA

Joshua is hooked on exploring space, from black holes to rogue planets! He likes to spend his free time reading or acting, and Mexican food always makes him smile.

CLARKE

Clarke loves playing video games and the piano—that is, when he's not busy working with the animals on his family's farm. He's also a champion spaghetti slurper!

ADELYNN

Adelynn has a huge imagination. It comes in handy when she's playing dress-up or creating one of her fabulous art pieces. Her friends call her Addie, and she loves learning about how things grow.

BEFORE YOU BEGIN . . .

Here are a few helpful hints!

1. This book is full of more than 150 mind-stretching and faith-building activities. If you need some help, you can find the answers on pages 168–187.

2. This symbol means the activity is a science experiment. You'll need a parent's permission and the items in the supplies list to complete the activity.

3. This book shares a lot of fun facts. You can discover even more about these topics in the Indescribable Kids devotionals. Just check out *Indescribable, How Great Is Our God,* and *The Wonder of Creation,* and look for the references to the devotionals under the activity titles. (Some of the activities offer brand-new information that's not from the devotionals.)

4. To find a type of activity, facts from a particular Indescribable Kids devotional, or a specific topic, check out the index on pages 166–167.

5. To learn more about the six Indescribable kids, visit https://www.indescribablekids.com.

Now, let's get started!

WHAT WiLL YOU CREATE?

To learn more about the creativity of God, check out devotion 1 in Indescribable.

This world began as a blank page. Actually, there wasn't even a page, just darkness and emptiness—and God! Then God filled it using His endless creativity (Genesis 1)! The space below is your own blank page to fill. Will you draw a new kind of animal, plant, or colorful scene? Or perhaps you'll write a story. What will you create?

MOUNTAIN MAZE

To learn more about Mount Everest, check out devotion 20 in Indescribable.

Mount Everest is the highest mountain in the world. It reaches 29,029 feet above sea level (that's about 5 ½ miles). Help Adelynn find the right path to the top.

WOULD YOU RATHER?

Would you rather hike to the tip-top of a snowy mountain or take a submarine down to the never-before-seen bottoms of the ocean?

Would you rather wrestle a giant polar bear or an angry octopus?

Would you rather eat ice cream in the snow on Mount Everest or try to sip a soda under the ocean?

THE EYES HAVE IT

To learn more about eyes, check out devotion 36 in Indescribable.

God designed the parts of your eyes to work together and create one of the most marvelous and exc-*eye*-ting senses you have—sight! Label the eye and discover the function of each part.

The **sclera**—or white of the eye—is the outer layer of the eye.

The **optic nerve** carries electrical impulses to the brain, where the brain turns those impulses into images.

The **iris** is the colorful part of the eye.

The **pupil** is the black center of the eye. It allows light to enter your eye.

The **lens** is behind the pupil and helps to focus light onto the retina.

The **ciliary muscles** help the lens focus and see things at different distances.

The **retina** is at the back of the eye and turns light into electrical impulses.

The **vitreous humor** is a thick fluid that fills the eye between the lens and the retina.

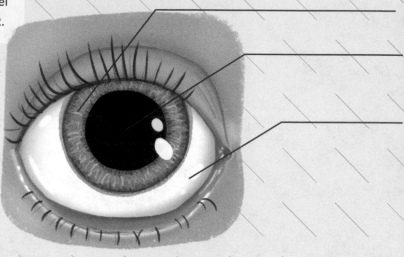

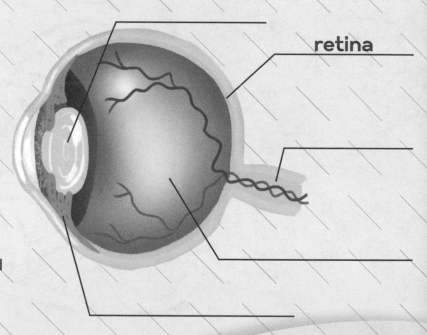

retina

DO YOU SEE WHAT I SEE?

Head to your backyard or a park and use your amazing sense of sight to see how many of these items you can find.

ANT
BIG ROCK
BIRD
BUTTERFLY
CLOUDS

FLOWERS
LEAF
ROOTS
SHADOW
SPIDERWEB

SQUIRREL
STICK
TREE
WORM

PUTTING THE PiECES ToGETHER

To learn more about the Deep Discoverer, check out devotion 1 in The Wonder of Creation.

The *Deep Discoverer*, a remote-controlled submarine, has photographed some amazing ocean creatures—like the "ghost-like" octopod and a bright red jellyfish scientists believe no one had ever seen before! With every trip, scientists fill in missing pieces of information about the ocean floor!

In Joshua's picture below, some pieces are missing. Complete the picture by writing the letter of the correct piece in each space.

God created our brains with the ability to use logic. That means we can solve a problem by carefully and calmly thinking about all the facts and then using those facts to come up with an answer.

Use logic to figure out the answer to this puzzle.

The Indescribable kids each adopted one pet, but none of them adopted the same kind of animal. Use the clues below to help you fill in the grid and figure out which pet belongs to which kid. (The first one is done for you.)

TO USE THE GRID

- Put an *X* in each box that is a wrong answer and an *O* in each box that is a right answer.

- For example: Read clue 1 below. Who wears glasses? Adelynn. Which pet has all black fur? The cat. That means Adelynn chose a cat. Put an *O* in the box where "Adelynn" and "cat" intersect. Next, put an *X* in the rest of Adelynn's row because logically, if she adopted the cat, she didn't adopt the other pets. Then put an *X* in the rest of the "cat" column because logically no one else chose a cat.

- Draw a line from each kid to the pet they picked!

CLUES

1. The kid who wears glasses adopted a pet with all black fur.

2. No boys adopted a dog.

3. No girls have a rabbit.

4. Evyn didn't choose a dog.

5. Neither Raz nor Joshua have a rabbit.

6. Neither Joshua nor Raz's pet can fly.

7. Joshua's pet has fur.

EVYN   RAZ   NORAH   JOSHUA   CLARKE   ADELYNN

	cat	dog	guinea pig	parakeet	gecko	rabbit
Evyn	X					
Raz	X					
Norah	X					
Joshua	X					
Clarke	X					
Adelynn	O	X	X	X	X	X

THE GREAT SPACE SEARCH

To learn more about the Apollo 11 mission, check out devotions 26 in Indescribable *and 78 in* How Great Is Our God.

In 1969, Neil Armstrong and Buzz Aldrin became the first people *ever* to walk on the Moon. To get there, they traveled over 238,000 miles on board the Apollo 11 spacecraft. That's like walking around the Earth 9 ½ times!

Every word in the list below is connected to the Apollo 11 mission. Can you find them all?

```
M  H  V  N  I  R  D  L  A  Z  Z  U  B  Y  S
O  Y  T  I  V  A  R  G  X  S  B  S  A  R  S
O  C  Q  F  G  X  V  A  X  Z  T  S  E  N  S
N  H  I  O  U  K  E  S  D  S  A  T  I  O  P
L  T  J  M  O  Y  T  A  I  N  A  L  B  A  A
A  R  Z  S  M  E  P  T  S  R  L  J  C  E  C
N  A  N  Q  K  H  N  P  C  O  K  W  W  H  E
D  E  B  C  C  E  A  R  C  B  O  P  F  S  C
I  B  O  N  I  C  A  L  N  E  G  E  O  K  R
N  R  U  C  E  N  E  J  C  W  E  O  X  O  A
G  A  S  R  U  A  T  N  I  R  P  T  O  O  F
L  B  A  L  H  S  P  A  C  E  S  U  I  T  T
A  C  M  C  N  H  D  W  Z  M  O  O  N  Q  P
E  M  I  S  S  I  O  N  C  O  N  T  R  O  L
N  M  G  N  O  R  T  S  M  R  A  L  I  E  N
```

Buzz Aldrin	Lunar craters	NASA	Scientists
Earth	Michael Collins	Neil Armstrong	Space race
Footprint	Mission Control	Rocket	Space suit
Gravity	Moon		Spacecraft
Launchpad	Moon landing		

NOT QUITE THE SAME

To learn more about genes, check out devotion 87 in The Wonder of Creation.

Genes (sounds like *jeans*) are like God's little instruction books for living things. The information they contain decides whether an animal will have stripes or spots, feathers or fur—or whether you'll have your mom's nose or your dad's eyes.

Check out these groups of animals below. Circle the animal in each group that's just a little different.

BROWSE THE EYEBROWS

To learn more about eyebrows, check out devotion 62 in How Great Is Our God.

God gave us eyebrows to help express our emotions. Look in the mirror and make the expressions listed below. See how your eyebrows are positioned, then draw eyebrows on the faces to show the right emotion!

EVYN IS SURPRISED.

RAZ IS ANGRY.

CLARKE IS SUSPICIOUS.

LET'S FACE IT

What could be more fun than making faces? Making faces on *sugar cookies*!
Ask a grown-up to help and see how many different faces you can make!

Ingredients

- slice-and-bake sugar cookie dough
- 1 16-ounce container of vanilla frosting
- 1 16-ounce container of chocolate frosting
- food coloring of your choice

Tools

- knife
- cookie sheet
- cooling rack
- small bowls
- spoons
- plastic baggies
- scissors

Directions

1. Slice and bake the sugar cookie dough according to package instructions. When the cookies are done, set them on a cooling rack.

2. While cookies are cooling, divide the vanilla icing into small bowls—one bowl for each color you want to have. (The chocolate icing will be the brown.) Think brown, blue, or green for the eyes; brown, black, or red for eyebrows; and red for the mouth. Add food coloring to the vanilla icing, according to the package directions. Stir well.

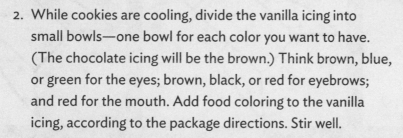

3. Scoop each frosting color into a separate plastic baggie and seal the top. Squeeze the frosting into one corner of the bag. Use scissors to snip off a small piece of the corner. Squeeze the bag so that the icing comes out in a line. Then make a face on each cookie! (Make sure cookies are completely cooled before decorating or the icing will melt.)

4. Share a few laughs, snap a few photos, and enjoy!

BLAST OFF!

To learn more about rockets and gravity, check out devotion 72 in How Great Is Our God.

Gravity is the invisible force that pulls an object *down* to another object—like how our feet are pulled down to Earth. Rockets overpower the pull of gravity by burning fuel. The burning fuel creates hot gases that blow out of the rocket so fast that they break the hold of gravity and push the rocket up into space.

Follow these steps to learn how to draw a rocket!

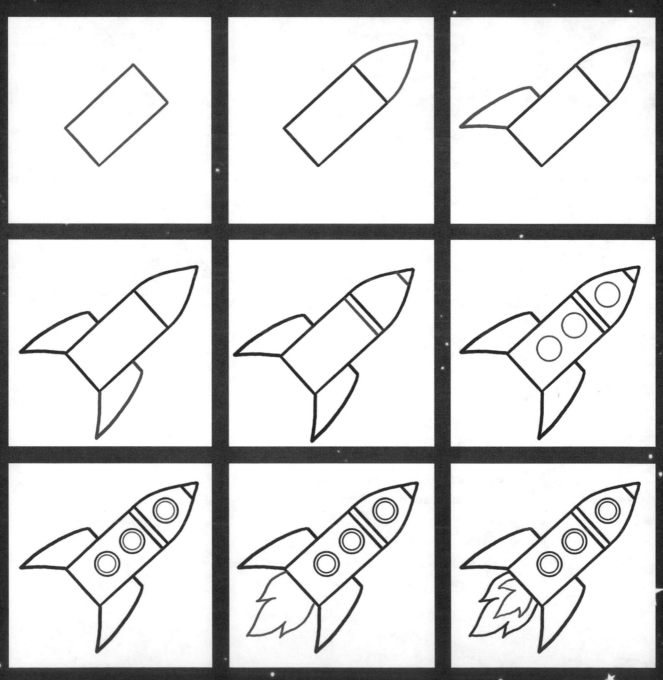

NOW DRAW A LARGE ROCKET ON THIS PAGE.

BEHIND THE SCENES

To learn more about "behind the scenes" workers, check out devotion 19 in The Wonder of Creation.

Missionaries live away from home and teach others about Jesus. But they don't work alone! Lots of people help them "behind the scenes," doing important things others don't see. But God sees! In fact, He uses "behind the scenes" people to do *big* things for His kingdom. And you can be one of them! Check out these ways you can help:

1 Choose a missionary your church supports and pray for them every day.

2 Be a pen pal to a missionary's kid—because it's tough being away from home and familiar things. Ask your parent or Sunday school teacher to help you connect with a missionary kid your age. Then write letters to each other, sharing about life where you each live.

3 Ask a missionary family what foods or items they miss most from home. Have a yard sale or a bake sale to raise money to send them those things.

4 When missionaries come for a visit, hang out with their kids your own age or offer to babysit their younger kids.

5 Look for businesses that use the money they make to help missionaries and other Christians in underdeveloped or war-torn countries. Ask your parents how your family can support these businesses.

GETTING FROM HERE TO THERE

Missionaries need to learn all they can about the new place where they'll be living. So they study maps to find out where everything is.

Imagine that a missionary is coming to your town. Where will they need to go? Think about places like church, the grocery store, school, and maybe even your house.

Create a map below showing the location of all those places. Add in your favorite spots too—like the park, movie theater, or ice cream shop!

To learn more about the layers of the ocean, check out devotion 48 in The Wonder of Creation.

God created the ocean to have layers. The top layer is the light-filled sunlight zone. Next come the twilight zone, midnight zone, and abyss. And at the very bottom are the trenches. No one knows what's down there!

Color these ocean layers. The deeper you go, the darker it gets!

IT'S A RIVER OF LIFE!

To learn more about rivers, check out devotion 99 in How Great Is Our God.

God gives us everything we need to grow strong in our faith. Kind of like the way a river gives plants, animals, and trees the nutrients they need to grow and be strong. That's why you'll see so much life around a river.

Take a close look at this river scene. Can you find all the life that's hidden in there?

ACORN
BLUE FLOWER
DUCK
GREEN APPLE

GREEN FROG
ORANGE DRAGONFLY
PURPLE MUSHROOM
RED FLOWER

SQUIRREL
SWAN
TWO BEAVERS
TWO LADYBUGS

WORM
YELLOW BUTTERFLY

WHAT'S UP ON MARS?

To learn more about Perseverance, *check out devotion 64 in* The Wonder of Creation.

Team up with a friend for this fill-in-the-blank fun.

Don't read the story yet! First, look at the list below and fill in each blank with the type of word listed. Next, add the words to the story, matching the numbered words to the numbered blanks. Then go back and read the whole story to find out what's up on Mars!

1. An animal: _____

2. Color: _____

3. An object: _____

4. Verb ending in -ed: _____

5. Verb ending in -ed: _____

6. Adjective: _____

7. Restaurant: _____

8. Verb ending in -ing: _____

9. Body part: _____

10. An object: _____

11. Body part: _____

12. A favorite food: _____

13. Color: _____

14. Verb ending in -ing: _____

15. Body part: _____

16. Piece of clothing: _____

17. Verb ending in -ing: _____

18. A noise ending in -ing: _____

19. Verb ending in -ed: _____

20. A number: _____

You probably already know that *Perseverance* landed on Mars on February 18, 2021. But scientists aren't talking about what happened next! Here's your super-secret, insider sneak peek:

Perseverance, that little robotic rover, was only about the size of a _____. But
                                                                        1

it was on a mission to explore the giant _____ _____. First,
                                                    2   **3**

it _____ up its engines. Then it _____ across the surface
        4   **5**

of the planet with _____ speed.
                            6

   At last it arrived at _____. It was just the right spot for _____.
                                7   **8**

Perseverance shot out its _____ to pick up a _____. It held
                                    9   **10**

it up close to its _____ and took a picture.
                            11

Then suddenly, *Perseverance* spotted the one thing it was really searching for—signs of

_____. There it was! A _____ _____
        12   **13**   **12**

just _____ on the ground. It had a long _____ and a
            14   **15**

strange-looking _____. It was _____ and _____ all
                        16   **17**   **18**

over the place! *Perseverance* _____ and took _____ pictures of that thing.
                                        19   **20**

   Scientists have always wondered if there was a _____ on Mars. And now they
                                                            12

know! (Sort of. Well, not really. But it sure makes a great story, right?)

21

HOME SWEET HOME

Habitat is another word for home. It's the place where a plant or animal lives. Its home—or habitat—includes things like shelter, food, water, weather, and even other plants and animals.

Match each of these animals to its habitat.

Soil

Orangutan

Beaver

Nest

Ocean

Duck

Cow

Desert

Rainforest

Clownfish

Baby bird

Arctic waters

Wetlands

Alligator

Meerkat

Dam

River

Worm

Narwhal

Pasture

HOLD ON!

To learn more about the seahorse, check out devotion 33 in Indescribable.

For a fish, the seahorse is a *terrible* swimmer. That's why God gave the seahorse its curly tail. That tail wraps around and holds on to underwater plants—so the seahorse doesn't get swept away by the ocean's currents!

Connect the dots below to make a seahorse.

Start here

God never changes (Malachi 3:6), but the seasons do! So how can you know what season it is? Be a detective like Evyn and look for clues! (Tip: If you live in a place that stays mostly warm or mostly cold all the time, pay extra attention to what the sun does.) Answer these questions to discover your clues. Then color the boxes that match the clues you find—and solve the mystery of what season it is!

1. What's the temperature outside? Is it hot or cold? Or somewhere in between?

    _____

2. Does the sun stay up until it's almost bedtime? Or is it dark before dinner is done?

    _____

3. Do the trees have leaves? Are the leaves just tiny buds? Are they big and green? Or are they red, orange, and gold?

    _____

4. Are flowers springing up, fully bloomed, or already gone?

    _____

5. How many animals and insects do you see? What are they doing?

    _____

	Temperatures	Sun	Trees	Flowers	Animals
Spring	Cool	Sets in the early evening	Leaves are tiny buds	Are just poking up through the dirt	Are waking up from winter
Summer	Hot	Sets in the late evening	Leaves are big and green	Are blooming	Are busy and all around
Fall	Cool	Sets in the early evening	Leaves are turning red, orange, and gold	Are fading	Eating extra to get ready for winter
Winter	Cold	Sets around dinnertime	Have dropped their leaves	Flowers are not blooming	Are hibernating or less active

What season is it? _____

CROSSING INTO SPACE

To learn more about space, check out devotions 1, 9, 25, and 38 in How Great Is Our God.

As scientists and astronauts study space, they're exploring places no person has ever been before. But even if we rocket to the ends of the universe, God will still be there with us (Psalm 139:7–12)!

Answer these questions to help Clarke fill in the crossword puzzle with fascinating space facts.

ACROSS
4. This reflects the Sun's light and shines at night.
6. The name of Earth's galaxy is pretty sweet. It's called the _____ _____ (2 words).

8. Parrots named Polly might want one of these, but astronauts can't have this crunchy snack.
9. Sailors use these twinkling lights in the sky to navigate across the ocean.

DOWN
1. The distance light travels in a year is called a _____-_____.
2. Earth's spot in space is just right for supporting life. Scientists named this spot after a fairy-tale girl who barged into a bear family's house!
3. The Earth travels around this star.
5. There's no air in space, so astronauts take tanks filled with _____ so they can breathe.
7. Earth has this, but space doesn't. That's why astronauts are *weightless*, which means they float!

BONES, BONES, BONES

To learn more about bones, check out devotion 9 in Indescribable.

There are 206 bones in the human body that join together to make up a skeleton.
Bones give our bodies their shape, protect our organs, and help us move.

Search through the letters below to find some of these bones. Then label the skeleton.

```
L M H U E W H T E L
U R A D I U S G A I
B L X C M U N T F W
S W N E I A C Z C K
V B R A L L U K S F
N U I A C G L Q S E
S K H R R K G F I M
Z P S A L T W D N U
H V W X A G O X X R
K F G X M I Z F M A
```

femur   radius   skull
humerus   ribs   ulna
phalange

SQUIGGLY, WIGGLY

To learn more about earthworms, check out devotion 50 in How Great Is Our God.

Earthworms may look like they're just wriggling around, but Norah has discovered they're actually churning up the soil. Nutrients that plants need get pushed to the top. And the worms' tunnels let air and water get down into the soil.

Help this little worm find its way through the maze and down to the deepest spot underground.

LOOK DEEPER

Sometimes important things don't look very important—like earthworms. That's why God never judges a person by the way they look. In fact, 1 Samuel 16:7 says this: "God does not see the same way people see. People look at the outside of a person, but the Lord looks at the heart."

SHEEP GOTTA HAVE A SHEPHERD

To learn more about sheep, check out devotion 41 in Indescribable.

There are seven differences in the two pictures below. Can you spot them all?

Sheep like to follow the crowd just about anywhere. They'll even follow other sheep off a cliff! That's why they need a shepherd to follow, just like we need Jesus, the Good Shepherd, to guide us to what is right.

GET ROOTED

To follow Jesus, you need faith. You can help your faith grow by getting "rooted" in God's Word—by reading it (Colossians 2:6–7). It's a lot like how a plant grows stronger by being rooted in soil and water. Check out this experiment to see what growing roots look like.

HOW TO "ROOT" A POTHOS PLANT

1. With a grown-up's help, cut off a 4-to-6-inch piece of a *pothos* (POH-thoss) plant with at least four leaves. (A pothos is a type of houseplant with heart-shaped leaves.)
2. Snip off the leaf closest to the cut end and place the stem in a glass of water.
3. Put the glass in a spot that gets lots of light but no direct sunlight.
4. Roots should start to appear over the next 30 days or so.
5. Once you see roots, wait 10 days before planting it in a small pot of dirt. Then watch your plant grow up strong!

GET THE PiCTURE?

To learn more about the Ranger missions to the Moon, check out devotion 96 in The Wonder of Creation.

Before Apollo 11 landed the first people on the Moon, the Ranger space probes were sent to do some exploring. But things didn't go as NASA planned. One of the first Rangers zoomed right past the Moon, another just didn't work, and two others lost all power!

Want to know which Ranger took the first close-up pictures of the Moon? Solve each Ranger's math problem and label the space probes below with the answer. The highest number is the Ranger that made it!

$2 \times 2 =$ 4

$2 + 3 =$

$2 + 2 + 2 =$

$6 + 1 =$

Ranger ☐ took the pictures!

OOPS!

We all fail sometimes—like so many of those Ranger missions. But God never asks us to be perfect. He just asks us to keep trusting and following Him (Romans 3:22–25).

A FRUITY PUZZLE

To learn more fruity facts, check out devotion 99 in Indescribable.

Fruits include apples, bananas, watermelons, and peas. Yep, peas! And peppers, squash, and cucumbers too. Because, scientifically speaking, a fruit is the part of the plant that has seeds.

Help Adelynn solve this *sudoku* (soo-DOH-koo) puzzle by filling in each square with a fruit. But wait! You must have an apple, banana, watermelon, and pepper in each row, column, and four-square box.

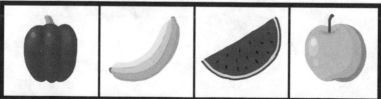

PLANTING SEEDS

When a fruit's seeds are planted, they grow into new plants. When you tell someone about God, it's like you're planting a "seed" of His truth. And this seed might grow into a new follower of Jesus (Mark 4:13–20)!

DEFINITELY NOT A BANANA

To learn more about the fruits of the Spirit, check out devotion 99 in Indescribable.

A banana might be a fruit, but it's not a fruit of the Spirit! Fruits of the Spirit don't grow on bushes or trees. They grow in your life when you live and love like Jesus did (Galatians 5:22–25)!

Match each fruit of the Spirit to its definition.

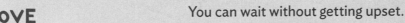

LOVE

JOY

PEACE

PATIENCE

KINDNESS

GOODNESS

FAITHFULNESS

GENTLENESS

SELF-CONTROL

You can wait without getting upset.

This is being thoughtful and nice to others.

This happy feeling lives in your heart, even when things aren't going your way.

This is the opposite of badness.

You are in control of what you do and say, even when you're upset or angry.

It's not just a feeling; it's the things you do. God wants your actions to show this—to Him and to your neighbors too.

This means you're loyal, you're dependable, and you keep your promises, just like God keeps His.

You are tender and kind—not harsh—with your words and actions.

This calm feeling comes from knowing God loves you and trusting Him to take care of you.

LIVING THE HIGH LIFE

To learn more about the amazing yak, check out devotion 11 in Indescribable.

Yaks live high in the Himalayan mountains—up to 20,000 feet (or over 3 ½ miles) above sea level. Temperatures can drop to 40 degrees below zero! But God gave yaks fur so thick that they can swim in icy ponds without getting cold!

Take a close look at these pictures. Which yak is different from all the rest?

MAKING ICE MOUNTAINS!

To learn more about the Himalayas, check out devotion 11 in Indescribable.

The Himalayas are called the "water towers" of Asia. That's because as the mountains' ice melts, it creates rivers of water for the lands below. Ice, or solid water, melts into liquid water when it's warmer than 32 degrees Fahrenheit. Water—or H_2O—also changes to steam at 212 degrees Fahrenheit. With a grown-up's help, try this experiment and make your own ice mountain!

Supplies
- clear plastic bottle
- water
- glass bowl
- cookie sheet
- ice cube

Steps

1. Fill the bottle with water and put it in the freezer on its side. Freeze for two hours. (It should be just beginning to freeze but not frozen solid. You'll know it's ready if ice crystals form when you move the bottle.)

2. Place the glass bowl upside down on the cookie sheet.

3. Put an ice cube on top of the upside-down glass bowl.

4. Slowly pour the water from the bottle onto the ice cube—and watch your ice mountain grow!

JUST ANOTHER DAY ON . . . MARS?!

To learn more about Mars and the other planets, check out devotion 83 in Indescribable.

Imagine you're one of the very first people to live on and explore Mars. Write a story about life on the Red Planet. Here are some ideas to get you started:

- How would your day start?
- What would you ride in to go exploring?
- What crazy thing would you find?
- What would you do for fun?

A MUSICAL MESSAGE

To learn more about how all creation sings, check out devotion 24 in Indescribable.

From birds to whales to stars, all God's creation sings His praises (Psalm 96:11–13)! And God wants you to praise Him with songs too (Psalm 96:1). So why not write your own song? After all, a song is simply words mixed with music to share a message. Grab a piece of paper and get started!

1. First, choose your message. What do you want to say? Maybe it's "God loves you," "God made everything amazing," or "God is indescribable!"

2. Next, think of words that rhyme with the words in your message, like *love* and *above*; or *you, new,* and *blue*; or *amazing, gazing,* and *praising*. Then, write two sentences that end with those words.

3. Think of two more words that rhyme and write two more sentences. Keep doing this until you've said all you want to say.

4. Now, add a tune. Make up your own tune or use one you already know, like "Twinkle, Twinkle, Little Star."

5. If you want an easy way to make one of your sentences longer, repeat a word (like *twinkle, twinkle*). Or add a word like "oh" or "yeah."

6. Finally, sing your song!

BUSY LiTTLE BRAiNS

To learn more about bees, check out devotion 25 in Indescribable.

A bee's brain weighs only about one milligram—that's less than the tiniest raindrop! But that little brain remembers which flowers have the best nectar and which direction to fly to find them.

How does your memory compare to a bee's? Grab a timer and set it for thirty seconds. Next, take a close look at this busy picture. When the timer dings, cover the picture with a piece of paper. Then see how many of the questions on the next page you can answer!

1. How many bees are buzzing around the picture?

_____

2. How many branches can you see on the tree?

_____

3. How many leaves are red?

_____

4. What's hanging off the tree branch (besides leaves)?

_____

5. How many flowers are in the picture?

_____

6. What color are the flowers?

_____

7. What color is Joshua's beekeeper outfit?

_____

8. Besides bees, what animals are in the picture?

_____

God created the bee's brain to learn and remember facts about flowers. And one of the things He created *your* brain to do is learn and remember His Word! Look up Psalm 119:97. Can you memorize the words?

COLORFUL CREATION

To learn more about the Caño Cristales River, check out devotion 81 in The Wonder of Creation.

From June to December, the *Macarenia clavigera* (mak-uh-RAY-nee-yuh kla-vee-JAIR-uh) blooms in shades of pink and red under the waters of the Caño Cristales River. Add in the river's yellow sand, green algae, and blue waters, and the river becomes a liquid rainbow!

Clarke is floating down the Caño Cristales River. Color in the spaces using the color code.

GARBAGE SOUP?

To learn more about the Great Pacific Garbage Patch, check out devotion 84 in How Great Is Our God.

Out in the Pacific Ocean, there's a swirling mass of garbage that's bigger than the state of Texas. It's called the Great Pacific Garbage Patch, but it's more like a garbage soup of fishing nets, bags, bottles, and bits of plastic. Ocean animals can get tangled in the mess, and some even mistake the plastic bags and other bits for food!

Oceans are important. They create over half the oxygen we breathe. They help control our weather. And they're home to billions of plants and animals. God put us in charge of keeping the world's oceans healthy (Genesis 1:26). Raz is doing his part. How can you help? Read the ideas below and mark three from the list to start doing this week.

❑ 1. Pretend you're a panda and use toothbrushes made from bamboo instead of plastic.

❑ 2. Carry your own washable fork and spoon to restaurants or other places that use throwaway utensils.

❑ 3. Use bar soap instead of liquids that come in plastic containers.

❑ 4. Ditch the straw or choose a paper or reusable one.

❑ 5. Snack on fresh fruit. It comes in its own natural packaging.

❑ 6. Skip the zip! Instead of plastic baggies, use cloth or reusable ones instead.

❑ 7. Tired of a toy? Don't trash it. Trade it or donate it.

❑ 8. Drink up—from water bottles you can refill again and again!

❑ 9. Donate or swap the clothes you outgrow.

❑ 10. Help with a river or beach cleanup.

❑ 11. Use cloth or reusable shopping bags instead of plastic.

❑ 12. Forget the balloons at your next party. Use paper decorations instead.

PiCTURES iN THE SKY

A *constellation* (kon-stuh-LAY-shuhn) is a group of stars that makes a picture in the sky. It's kind of like connect the dots, except with stars. One of the most famous constellations is the Big Dipper. Its seven stars form a giant ladle.

Create your own constellation—on paper. Use a pencil to lightly draw a simple animal, person, or shape. Try to use only straight lines to draw it. At each point where two lines meet, draw a star. Add other animals and shapes to make a whole nighttime scene!

People created pictures out of the stars, but God is the One who put each and every star in the sky—just exactly where He wanted them to be (Psalm 8:3 NIV).

WHEN YOU'RE HAPPY AND YOU KNOW IT

*To learn more about cats and their **purr**-sonalities, check out devotion 3 in How Great Is Our God.*

Adelynn knows her cats are happy and content—because they're purring! What should you do when you're feeling happy and content? Laugh, smile, do a little dance, and praise God! Because every good thing we have comes from Him (James 1:17)!

Use the word bank to fill in the answers to the crossword clues. (Hint: You won't need to use all the words.)

CAT	COUGAR	LEOPARD	MANE	PAWS	ROAR	TIGER
CLAWS	KITTEN	LION	MEOW	PURR	TAIL	WHISKERS

ACROSS

4. The fluffy fur around a male lion's head is called a _____.
5. Cats use the _____ on their faces to feel their way through tight spaces.
7. The _____ is a big cat with orange, black, and white stripes.
8. The _____ lives in the jungle and is known for its spots.
10. A lion's _____ can be heard up to five miles away!

DOWN

1. Cats use their _____ to defend themselves and climb trees.
2. Cats say _____.
3. When a cat is angry, it often twitches its _____.
6. A baby cat is a _____.
9. When cats are happy, they _____.

41

DON'T BREAK A SWEAT

To learn more about sweat, check out devotion 13 in How Great Is Our God.

All that exercise is making Norah sweaty! Did you know emotions can make you sweaty too? Like when you're nervous, scared, or worried. Don't sweat it out on your own. Tell God what's worrying you (1 Peter 5:7)!

There's no need to sweat this test. Just write *T* next to each true statement and *F* next to each false one.

_____ 1. Sweat is your body's way of keeping you cool.

_____ 2. Sweat is made by your nose hairs.

_____ 3. Most of your sweat glands are located on your elbows.

_____ 4. Hippos have pink sweat.

_____ 5. You have between 10 and 12 sweat glands in your whole body.

_____ 6. Sweat can happen when you're exercising, nervous, or sick.

_____ 7. Eating spicy foods can make you sweat.

SWEAT IT OUT

Sweat out those emotions and extra energy with a little exercise.

BEAR WALK—Bend over and put your hands on the floor and your bottom in the air. How fast can you walk across the floor on all fours?

CRAB CRAWL—Sit with your knees bent and feet flat on the floor in front of you. Place your hands on the floor behind you. Lift up your bottom and "crawl" like a crab.

TURTLE SWIM—Lie facedown on the floor with your arms stretched out in front of you. Lift your arms and legs up off the floor. Kick your feet while moving your arms down to your sides and then back up again—just like you're swimming. How long can you "swim"?

BUNNY HOP SQUATS—Stand with your feet apart. Bend at the knees to squat down, keeping your back straight. Then quickly straighten your legs and jump up. How high can you jump?

LiONS, HiPPOS, AND GORiLLAS—OH MY!

To learn more about the Congo Basin, check out devotion 16 in The Wonder of Creation.

Africa's Congo Basin is rich in animals, like lions, elephants, and gorillas. And it's rich in resources, like rubber, copper, and gold. But God's love and mercy are a treasure bigger than any elephant and greater than all the world's gold (Lamentations 3:22–23)!

Search through the letters below. Can you find all these animals and resources from the Congo Basin?

```
D  D  Y  T  Q  B  W  H  E  T  I  M  B  E  R
J  I  R  A  I  K  B  A  L  W  B  A  E  J  G
W  L  A  A  L  N  H  G  E  W  O  L  V  S  W
W  M  V  M  P  T  V  H  P  C  U  O  P  X  V
A  M  C  R  O  O  I  L  H  C  O  P  P  E  R
D  T  M  V  N  N  E  H  A  F  D  R  M  E  Z
Q  W  O  Z  D  X  D  L  N  Q  T  N  B  X  Y
Y  W  T  O  S  R  B  S  T  U  Q  B  X  Z  N
U  A  L  L  I  R  O  G  D  N  U  K  Z  L  Y
B  W  D  R  D  I  B  J  V  R  J  N  Z  S  D
L  Y  F  C  N  G  M  P  Q  I  X  D  D  C  N
V  C  G  S  O  S  B  J  N  K  K  S  S  U  J
L  Z  K  L  I  D  B  W  J  M  T  Y  F  X  Z
A  J  D  C  L  R  W  P  I  Q  C  A  N  F  Y
P  U  K  I  K  O  H  T  C  R  F  K  F  E  A
```

COPPER	ELEPHANT	GORiLLA	LiON	TIMBER
DiAMONDS	GOLD	LEOPARD	RUBBER	TiN

43

SUITED FOR SPACE

To learn more about space suits, check out devotion 89 in The Wonder of Creation.

Space suits keep astronauts safe when they're walking in space, so each part has a purpose. Read the diagram below, then grab a piece of paper and draw each part of the space suit.

The "shirt" piece hooks up to all the life-support equipment.

Sleeves attach to the shirt. The outer layer is water resistant, bulletproof, and fire resistant.

Gloves have tiny heaters inside to keep fingers warm.

The pants have rings along the waist so that astronauts can hook themselves to the spacecraft.

The bodysuit is super-stretchy and filled with tiny tubes of running water to keep astronauts cool.

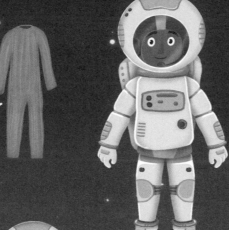

Boots are super-strong and made for walking on rocky ground.

The whole suit is topped off with a helmet. There's even a little foam block for nose scratching in there!

A cloth cap has a microphone and earphones for communicating with other astronauts.

The backpack holds oxygen for breathing, the radio, and other important equipment.

Like all those space suit parts, God has a purpose—a job—for every person every day (Ephesians 2:10). Stick close to God, talk to Him, and He'll show you what He wants you to do today.

MAKE A SPACE SUIT

Ready to blast off into space? You'll need a space suit first! Grab some boxes, paper plates, tape, crayons, scissors, glue, and any other supplies you might need—and make your own. (Ask a grown-up to help cut the cardboard.) Here are some of Raz's ideas to get you started:

- Cut an opening in one side of a box to make a helmet.

- Cut arm and neck holes in a large box for the body.

- Glue on bottle caps to make buttons and dials.

- Draw, color, and cut out your own NASA mission patches, then tape them to your suit.

- Make a life-support backpack from a paper-covered cereal box.

SNIFF, SNIFF!

To learn more about animals' noses, check out devotions 47 and 95 in How Great Is Our God.

Dogs use their noses to put together a picture of the world—that's why they sniff *everything*!

Each nostril can smell separately. That gives the dog two different "pictures" of the world around it. It's almost like dogs can smell in 3D!

Finish this doggie's face by using a pencil to draw a mirror image of the picture.

Like dogs, we use our senses to help us find our way through the world. But sometimes we need extra help. That's why God gave us His Word—to help us find our way (Psalm 119:105).

JUST ONE WAY

To learn more about rogue planets, check out devotion 45 in The Wonder of Creation.

God made the eight planets in our solar system to *orbit*, or circle, around the Sun. They follow the same path every trip. But other planets, out in the Milky Way Galaxy, go a different way every time. They're called *rogue* (ROHG) planets.

Check out this picture of the solar system. Use the words below to label the Sun and all the planets. Even that rogue one.

EARTH	MARS	NEPTUNE	SATURN	URANUS
JUPITER	MERCURY	ROGUE PLANET	SUN	VENUS

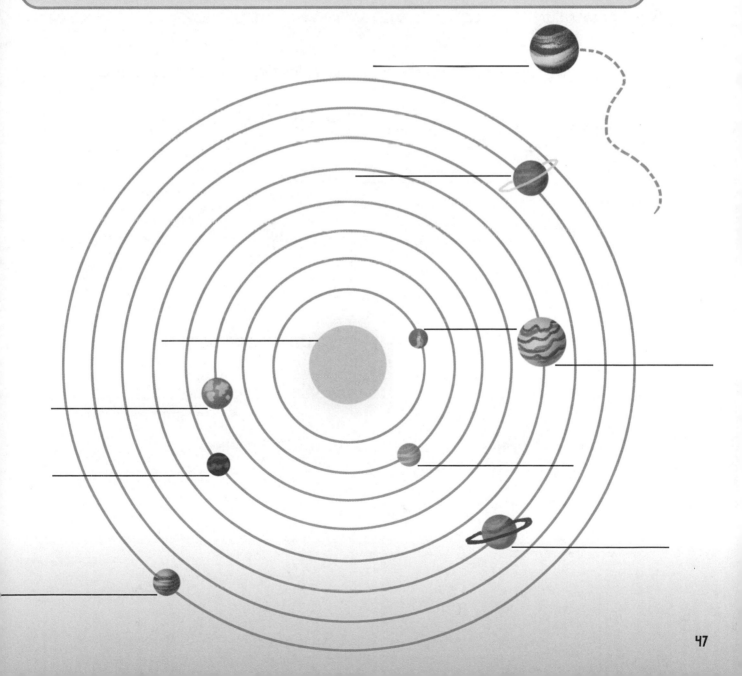

WHEN ARE WE?!?

Team up with a friend for this fill-in-the-blank fun. Don't read the story yet! First, fill in each blank with the type of word listed. Next, add the words to the story, matching the numbered words to the numbered blanks. Then go back and read the whole story to find out what happened when!

1. Something used in crafts: _____

2. Type of tool (plural): _____

3. Something small (plural): _____

4. Funny noise ending in -ing: _____

5. Verb: _____

6. Silly sound effect ending in -ed: _____

7. Adjective: _____

8. Kitchen appliance (plural): _____

9. Verb ending in -ing: _____

10. Animal sound ending in -ed: _____

11. Funny sound ending in -ing: _____

12. Future year: _____

13. Verb ending in -ed: _____

14. Adjective: _____

15. A huge machine: _____

16. Color: _____

17. Vegetable: _____

18. Favorite dessert: _____

19. A number between 1 and 10: _____

20. Verb ending in -ing: _____

21. A silly name for a pet: _____

22. A verb ending in -ed: _____

Adelynn and I were working on a science project at school. We were figuring out a new way to tell time. Our invention was covered in ＿＿＿＿＿＿ and ＿＿＿＿＿＿ and ＿＿＿＿＿＿. But we
1 **2** **3**

must have crossed some wires because there was a loud ＿＿＿＿＿＿ noise. The whole room
4

started to ＿＿＿＿＿＿ and then—*POW!*
5

Adelynn and I ＿＿＿＿＿＿ and looked around. We were still at school, but everything was
6

＿＿＿＿＿＿! All the kids were wearing ＿＿＿＿＿＿ instead of backpacks. One classroom
7 **8**

wall was a giant screen showing robots ＿＿＿＿＿＿. Just then, the bell ＿＿＿＿＿＿. All
9 **10**

the kids started ＿＿＿＿＿＿ into the hall. We decided to follow.
11

We wound up in the lunchroom. There on the wall was a lunch menu for Tuesday, March 4,

＿＿＿＿＿＿! What? We had ＿＿＿＿＿＿ ourselves into the future! We hurried to grab
12 **13**

some lunch, which came out of a ＿＿＿＿＿＿ ＿＿＿＿＿＿. You just pushed a button and
14 **15**

out popped a ＿＿＿＿＿＿ ＿＿＿＿＿＿ ＿＿＿＿＿＿. We gave it a rating of
16 **17** **18**

＿＿＿＿＿＿ out of 10 stars.
19

After lunch, we knew we had to get back to our time. We hurried back to our science project,

but a robot was ＿＿＿＿＿＿ with it. She was a teacher, and her name was Ms. ＿＿＿＿＿＿.
20 **21**

We explained what happened, and she ＿＿＿＿＿＿. Suddenly the ＿＿＿＿＿＿ sound
22 **4**

started again and . . . *POW!* We were back in our time again. There was just one problem.

Ms. ＿＿＿＿＿＿ had come with us!
21

DON'T WASTE A MINUTE

To learn more about night and day, check out devotion 75 in How Great Is Our God.

Scientists define a day as how long it takes the Earth to spin completely around. That's 24 hours, right? Well, actually, each day on Earth is 23 hours, 56 minutes, and 4.09 seconds long.

While some places have more daylight and others have more night, we all have the same amount of time to live out each day. And we don't want to waste a minute of it!

The Bible tells us to "be a light" that helps other people see God (Matthew 5:16). In other words, spend time every day shining God's love into the world. Read the ideas below, then check off each act of kindness after you complete it. But be sure to get a parent's permission first!

☐ **1.**
When you see a friend or neighbor, smile, wave, and say hello!

☐ **2.**
Draw a happy picture or write a friendly message on the sidewalk in front of your home using chalk.

☐ **3.**
If an older neighbor has a dog, offer to take it for a walk.

☐ **4.**
If a family friend has small children, offer to play with them for an hour or two.

☐ **5.**
Are your parents putting away groceries? Offer to help!

☐ **6.**
Visit or call a grandparent and chat for a while.

☐ **7.**
Surprise someone with a bundle of wildflowers on their porch.

☐ **8.**
Bake cookies, bag them up, and share them with all your friends and neighbors.

☐ **9.**
Meet a new kid at school? Offer to introduce them to your friends.

☐ **10.**
If you see a neighbor working outside, take them a cup of cold water in the summer or hot chocolate in the winter.

WATCH OUT FOR FALLING APPLES!

To learn more about gravity, check out devotion 47 in Indescribable.

Gravity is a force that pulls two objects together—like your feet and the ground or a slinky and the next step on the stairs. Sir Isaac Newton discovered gravity about 300 years ago when—according to legend—an apple fell on his head!

Gravity pulls on everything with the same force. So if you drop two different objects at the same time, they'll hit the ground at the same time. Unless air gets in the way! When an object is lighter, fluffier, or more spread out, air can slow its fall. That's called *air resistance,* or *drag.* Test it out by setting up a race between these different objects. Which hits the ground first?

Supplies

- a rock
- cotton ball
- paper clip
- book
- shoe
- pencil
- a wadded-up sheet of notebook paper
- a flat sheet of notebook paper

RACE 1

rock vs. cotton ball

Which do you think will win?

_____

Actual winner:

_____

RACE 2

paper clip vs. book

Which do you think will win?

_____

Actual winner:

_____

RACE 3

shoe vs. pencil

Which do you think will win?

_____

Actual winner:

_____

RACE 4

wadded-up paper vs. flat paper

Which do you think will win?

_____

Actual winner:

_____

WHAT DID YOU OBSERVE?

_____

_____

_____

51

LiFE iN THE TREES

To learn more about orangutans and other animals, check out devotion 85 in How Great Is Our God.

God made orangutans to live almost their entire lives high up in the rainforest trees of Borneo and Sumatra. Both their hands and feet can grab and hold on to branches, so they can swing easily from tree to tree.

Map out this orangutan's move through the trees by following this order:

"Swing" from square to square—up, down, or across, but not diagonally—to get to the finish line.

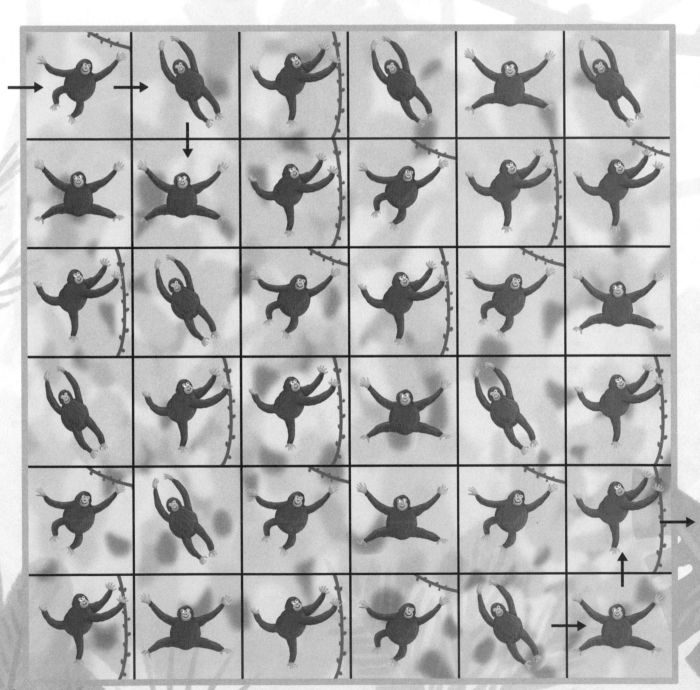

ANIMALS EVERYWHERE!

Scientists estimate there are between 1 and 2 million different animal species on Earth. They divide all these animals into two big groups: *vertebrates* (VUR-tuh-brayts) with backbones and *invertebrates* (in-VUR-tuh-brayts) without backbones. Draw a line to match each animal to the animal group it belongs to.

VERTEBRATES

AMPHIBIANS can live on both land and water.

BIRDS are the only animals that have feathers. They hatch from hard-shelled eggs. Many birds can fly, but not all.

FISH live in water and use gills to breathe. Their skin is covered in scales. Fins help them swim and steer their way through the water.

MAMMALS have fur or hair, and the babies drink their mother's milk.

REPTILES lay eggs and have scales or plates instead of hair or fur.

INVERTEBRATES

ARACHNIDS have eight legs. Their bodies have two parts: the head and the abdomen.

CRUSTACEANS have hard shells, and most live underwater. Many have claws on their front limbs for grabbing things.

INSECTS have six legs. Their bodies are made up of three parts: the head, thorax (middle part), and abdomen (the end).

SPONGES live underwater. They have no heads, eyes, tails, or even mouths! Instead, their bodies are filled with tiny holes. As water flows through the holes, they filter out little bits of food.

Scientists don't know exactly how many animals there are on Earth, but God does. He even knows every sparrow that flies and falls (Matthew 10:29 NIV). And there are more than 1.6 billion sparrows!

THAT'S NO STAR!

To learn more about shooting stars, check out devotion 82 in The Wonder of Creation.

Evyn and Joshua are watching for shooting stars. But are shooting stars really stars?
Find out by using the words from the word bank to fill in the blanks below.

ASTEROIDS	DUST	LIGHT	WISH
ATMOSPHERE	GOD	METEOR	

Have you ever seen a shooting star? It's a quick streak of _____ that zips across
1

the nighttime sky. The thing is, that shooting star isn't a star at all. It starts as a meteoroid,

which is a piece of rock in outer space. Some are as tiny as a piece of _____.
2

Others are up to 330 feet in size—or just a little smaller than a football field. (Larger objects

are called _____.)
3

When a meteoroid crashes into Earth's _____, it begins to burn up. That's
4

what causes the bright streak of light, and that's when the meteoroid's name changes to

_____, or shooting star.
5

Some people say you can wish on a shooting star, but it's just a game.

Stars can't help you. But _____ can. He
6

listens to every word you say, and He answers every

single prayer. His answers might not always be exactly

what you _____ for, but they will always
7

be just what you need (Isaiah 65:24; Psalm 37:4–5).

A LEAFY ARRANGEMENT

To learn more about leaves and how they change colors, check out devotion 69 in How Great Is Our God.

God gave trees a way to make their own food with a chemical called *chlorophyll* (KLOHR-uh-fil). Chlorophyll gives leaves their green color. In fall, trees stop making chlorophyll, so the green disappears—and the red, yellow, and orange come shining through!

In the grid below, there's a special group of four leaves that looks like this:

How fast can you find it?

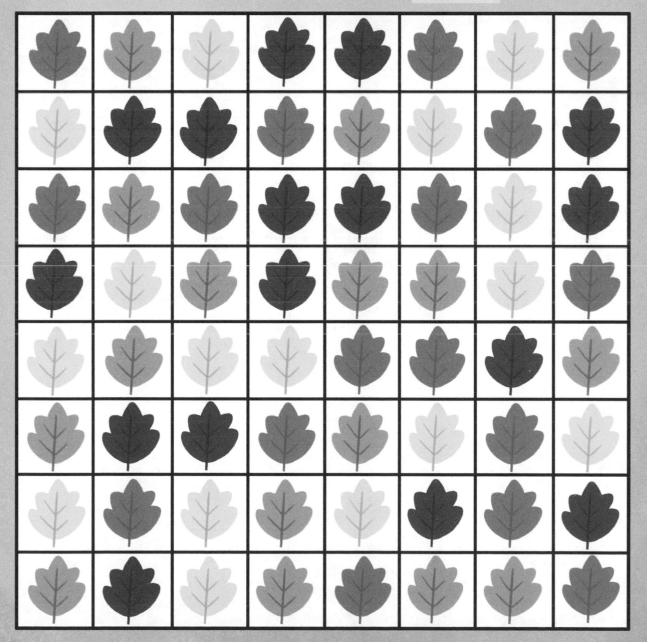

BY THE NUMBERS

To learn more about the Sierra redwoods, check out devotion 70 in How Great Is Our God.

California has some of the oldest trees around. They're called Sierra redwoods—and some were even alive when Jesus was born!

Solve the math problems below and fill in the blanks to find out how old these trees are and how tall they can grow.

Many Sierra redwood trees are between ___,000 and ___,000 years old!
                                               D   B

Some trees might even be over ___,000 years old!
                                C

These amazing trees can grow to be ___ oo feet tall—that's about as tall as the Statue of Liberty!
                                        B

And unless you have *really* long arms, you can't hug these trees. That's because their trunks can

be more than ___ ___ feet around!
               A   C

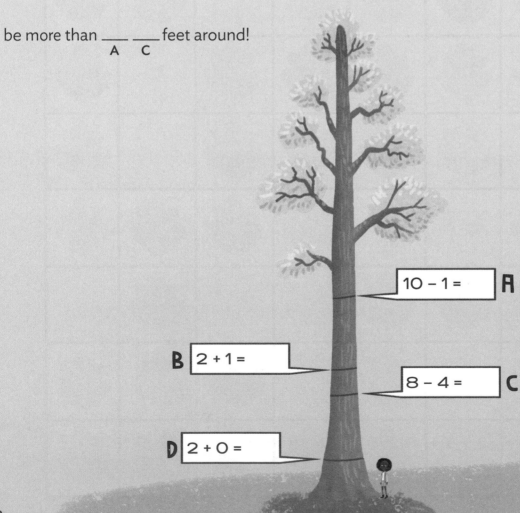

B | $2 + 1 =$

D | $2 + 0 =$

$10 - 1 =$ | A

$8 - 4 =$ | C

TO THE MOON . . . AGAIN!

The Orion spacecraft was built to fly NASA astronauts to the Moon,
allowing them to spend a week exploring the Moon's surface!

Color this rocket's trip to the Moon.

BUILD A SUNDIAL

To learn more about sundials, check out devotion 92 in How Great Is Our God.

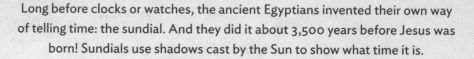

Long before clocks or watches, the ancient Egyptians invented their own way of telling time: the sundial. And they did it about 3,500 years before Jesus was born! Sundials use shadows cast by the Sun to show what time it is.

Follow these steps with Clarke to build your own sundial. (Make sure to do this experiment on a clear, sunny day.)

Supplies

- paper plate
- a new and unsharpened pencil
- tape
- markers or crayons
- a watch or clock
- a book, water bottle, or large stone

Steps

1. Tape the pencil, standing up, to the center of the plate.

2. Place the plate in a sunny spot outside. Do you see the pencil's shadow? (If there are too many clouds, you may need to try again on a sunnier day.)

3. Use a marker or crayon to trace the pencil's shadow.

4. Check your watch or clock to see what time it is. Write that time next to the line.

5. Use a book, water bottle, or large stone to anchor the plate in place. You don't want the wind to move it around!

6. Wait about an hour, then repeat steps 3 and 4. Try to do this several times throughout the day to fill in the times on your sundial.

IT'S TIME FOR JOKES!

What time is spelled the same forward and backward?   *Noon*

What time is it when you can't read a clock?   *Time to get glasses!*

What question can you ask all day long and get a different answer that is always the right answer?   *What time is it?*

MOON ON THE MOVE

To learn more about Titan, check out devotion 5 in The Wonder of Creation.

In each fact below, there's a scrambled word. Unscramble the word, and then circle it in the word search.

Earth isn't the only planet in our solar system that has a **onom** _____. In fact,
1

nturaS _____ has 82 moons! One of them is called **itTna** _____, and
2   3

astronomers have discovered that it's drifting away from Saturn! The spacecraft Cassini spent

13 years taking pictures while in **birot** _____ around Saturn. Those pictures helped
4

tromasoners _____ figure out that Titan is drifting a whole four inches away
5

from Saturn every year!

```
E  I  D  L  K  Z  Y  S  H  S  W
P  N  W  L  X  D  V  P  M  R  X
W  M  Y  D  G  S  G  G  S  E  A
D  N  A  T  I  T  A  P  D  M  F
I  P  O  C  R  S  A  W  Y  O  E
F  Q  V  X  A  T  H  B  M  N  W
P  F  V  T  T  G  H  M  O  O  C
V  U  U  Q  E  I  N  U  O  R  S
D  R  B  O  U  O  B  K  N  T  Z
N  R  S  D  Q  B  P  R  K  S  U
T  O  Z  L  L  J  K  U  O  A  H
```

DEEP INTO THE DEEP BLUE SEA

To learn more about the Deep Discoverer, *check out devotion 1 in* The Wonder of Creation.

Imagine you're the scientist in charge of the *Deep Discoverer*, a remote-controlled submarine that can dive over 19,000 feet into the ocean. That's over 3 ½ miles deep! Finish writing this story in the log (a kind of journal for sailors) about what you discover.

DAILY LOG

Today was my third day exploring the ocean with the *Deep Discoverer.* I was studying this cluster of coral when—out of the corner of my eye—I saw something glowing in the distance. I steered the *Deep Discoverer* toward it. Suddenly, out of the darkness . . .

God is so big and amazing that we'll never know everything about Him (Isaiah 55:8–9). But you can discover something new every time you dive into His Word. Go ahead and give it a try!

GOING DEEP!

To learn more about the Deep Discoverer check out devotion 1 in The Wonder of Creation.

Take a close look at this picture of Joshua's diving adventure. Can you find all the hidden pictures?

DO YOU SEE THAT?

To learn more about optical illusions, check out devotion 34 in The Wonder of Creation.

Your eyes *see* the images around you, but God created your brain to tell you *what* you're seeing. Because you see so much, your brain creates shortcuts to quickly decide what you're seeing. *Optical illusions* (OP-ti-kuhl ih-LOO-zhuhnz) use light, color, pattern, and even movement to trick your brain into taking the wrong shortcut!

Make Your Own Optical Illusion

Turn two pictures into one with this simple optical illusion.

Supplies

- white cardstock
- scissors
- pencil
- markers
- clear tape

Steps

1. Cut two 3-by-3-inch squares of cardstock.

2. In the center of one square, use a pencil to draw a birdcage.

3. In the center of the other square, draw a bird. Make sure the bird is smaller than the birdcage.

4. Trace both drawings with a black marker, then color the bird.

5. Tape the pencil's end to the blank side of one card. Tape the other card on top. Make sure both pictures are showing. Tape all around the edges of the cards.

6. Hold the pencil between your hands and rub your hands together to make the pictures spin.

What happens to the bird?

_____

_____

_____

_____

MADE TO PRAY

Prayer is simply talking to God, and it's one of the things He created you
to do (1 Thessalonians 5:16–18). There's no right or wrong way to pray.
You can whisper your prayer, shout it, or even write it in a letter.

Use this space to write out your own prayer to God—just like Adelynn is doing. Here are
some ideas to get you started:

- Thank God for the good things in your life.
- Ask Him for the things you need.
- Ask Him what you can do for Him.
- Ask Him to help others and to show you how to help them too.

Dear God,

_____

_____

_____

_____

_____

_____

_____

In Jesus' name, amen.

SEEDS ON THE SEA

To learn more about seeds, check out devotion 5 in How Great Is Our God.

God created different ways to spread seeds. Some are spread by animals. Others are spread by exploding seedpods (yes, exploding!), and some—like the coconut—spread by floating on the sea!

Take a look at these two pictures of Norah's boogie-board adventure. They might look alike, but they're not. There are seven differences. Can you spot them all?

WOULD YOU RATHER?

Would you rather boogie board with dolphins or sail on a pirate ship?

Would you rather ride on the back of a cheetah or fly on the back of a bird?

Would you rather live on a deserted island or in the desert with your best friend?

Would you rather have a lion's mane or a horse's tail?

IT'S A GERM INVASION!

To learn more about germs, check out devotion 93 in How Great Is Our God.

Germs are tiny organisms that constantly try to sneak into eyes, noses, cuts, and scrapes. They attack and try to make us sick. But God gave us an immune system to zap these sneaky little invaders!

Take a close look at these "germs." Do you see the pattern? Fill in the blanks with the missing germ to complete the pattern.

FUZZY, FURRY, FEATHERED FRIENDS

Pets are animals that live with us. They aren't used for work. And they aren't raised for food, like cows and chickens. Dogs are the most popular pets, but people also keep cats, birds, lizards, and even axolotls (happy-looking salamanders that live in lakes).

Solve the sudoku puzzle by filling in each square with an animal face. But wait! There's a rule: you must include a cat, dog, bunny, and bird in each row, each column, and each four-square box.

NATURAL TREASURES

To learn more about God's creation, check out devotion 30 in Indescribable.

God created massive stars and mighty mountains. But He also created butterfly wings, whirligig seeds, and wildflowers. Go exploring like Norah and collect some of God's smallest creations. Then create a mobile to display the treasures you find!

Supplies

- small treasures from nature, such as pinecones, acorns, strips of bark, wildflowers, and leaves
- scissors
- string or yarn
- a sturdy and interesting stick, about 12 inches long
- tape

Steps

1. Ask a parent to help you go exploring in your backyard, a park, or a nearby forest.

2. Collect acorns, small rocks or shells, leaves, whirligig seeds, and other small treasures from God's creation.

3. Cut a piece of string about 12 inches long. Tie one end around the stick and tie or tape a treasure to the other end.

4. Repeat for each treasure in your collection. Use different lengths of string to create a mobile to hang in your room.

OUTDOOR CHALLENGES!

1. Use leaves, sticks, or rocks to spell out your name or make the shape of a heart.

2. Lie on a blanket and search for shapes in the clouds.

3. Go on a bug hunt. How many different bugs can you find?

SCARY FAST!

To learn more about sharks, check out devotion 59 in Indescribable.

Sharks are fast swimmers—scary fast! Most sharks can zoom along at 20–30 miles per hour, but the mako shark can swim more than 60 miles an hour! That's as fast as a car on a freeway!

Follow these steps to learn how to draw a shark.

NOW DRAW A LARGE SHARK ON THIS PAGE.

THE GREAT *WHAT?*

To learn more about the Great Conjunction, check out devotion 100 in The Wonder of Creation.

What's the Great Conjunction? Use the word bank below to fill in the blanks and find out!

GREAT	**MILLION**	**SOLAR SYSTEM**	**TWENTY**
JUPITER	**ORBIT**	**SUN**	

God set every planet in our _____ in its place. And He told them exactly how fast to
1

_____, or circle, around the _____. It takes Saturn about 30 years to orbit the
2   3

Sun, while _____ makes the trip in only 12 years. Once every _____ years,
4   5

Saturn catches up, and that's called the _____ Conjunction (cuhn-JUNK-shun). The two
6

planets look like they're side by side in the sky, but they're really 456 _____ miles apart!
7

SPACE MAZE

Can you find your way through the maze of space? Start at the Sun. Be sure
to pass through Earth and Jupiter before landing on Saturn.

SMALL BUT POWERFUL!

To learn more about cells, check out devotion 2 in How Great Is Our God.

Read about the basic parts of all living things. Then answer the questions below.

God made the heavens, the Earth, and every living thing (Genesis 1). When we study science—like Raz—we discover some of the amazing details about His creation, like cells, proteins, *peptides* (PEP-tides), and *amino* (uh-MEE-no) acids.

Cells are the basic parts that make up all living things. Inside every cell are proteins. Different proteins do different jobs, like fight off diseases and digest food. Proteins are made up of chains of peptides, and peptides are made up of chains of even smaller amino acids.

The human body has about 20 different amino acids. But they mix, match, and join together to make thousands of different peptides—which mix, match, and join together to create thousands of different proteins.

The chances of all those amino acids, peptides, and proteins *accidentally* mixing, matching, and joining together to make the human body are about 1 in 10 duodecillion. That's a 1 with 40 zeros after it! Sound impossible? Not for God. He can do anything!

1. Which chapter of the Bible tells about God creating the heavens, the Earth, and all living things?

_____

2. What are two jobs that proteins do?

_____

_____

3. What are peptides made up of?

_____

4. What are the chances that the human body could just "happen" by accident?

_____

5. God put all those amino acids, peptides, proteins, and cells together in just the right combinations to make you. What does that say about His power and how much He cares about you?

_____

_____

ADVENTURE IN THE MOUNTAINS!

To learn more about Sherpas, check out devotion 7 in The Wonder of Creation.

Imagine you're climbing Mount Everest with Raz and a Sherpa as your guide. The Sherpa is an expert climber and knows the best way up the mountain because he lives nearby. Finish writing the story below and tell what happens next!

Dear Diary,

Raz and I have lost our Sherpa. And we really need him because there aren't any signs up here to tell us which way to go. You see, we stopped to check out this really cool-looking ice cave. But somehow our ropes broke, and then . . .

THE GOLDILOCKS ZONE

To learn more about the Goldilocks Zone, check out devotion 1 in How Great Is Our God.

Adelynn has discovered that Earth sits in the sweet spot—the perfect place—in space. Scientists call this spot the *Habitable Zone*, or the *Goldilocks Zone*. That's because it's in the sweet spot where all the conditions are *juuust* right for life. Unscramble the words in the sentences below to discover what makes Earth's spot in space just right.

1. Earth is just the right idsctaen _____ from the Sun, so it doesn't get too hot or too cold.

2. There is liquid trwae _____ and lots of it!

3. Earth is made of ckor _____ instead of gas like Jupiter and Neptune.

4. The magnetosphere and the oozen _____ layer act like sdhelsi _____ to protect the Earth from the Sun's harmful rays.

5. The mosatereph _____ has just the right combination of gases for breathing.

6. The ooMn _____ slows down the spin of the Earth and gives us a 24-hour day.

7. The Sun is a single star. Its teah _____ and ghtli _____ stay about the same all the time.

8. The planet piJuret _____ acts like a vacuum cleaner and sweeps up rogue asteroids, comets, and meteors so they don't hit Earth.

9. The neplats _____ in our solar system stay in their set orbits.

10. Earth is in a calm spot in the kliMy yaW _____ _____ Galaxy, where it's not too crowded by other stars and planets.

JUST THE RiGHT SPOT

The chances of another planet meeting all the conditions of the Goldilocks Zone and being perfect for life are 1 in 700 quintillion, or 1 in 700,000,000,000,000,000,000. In other words, God made the Earth and put it in just the right spot for life (Isaiah 45:18).

IMPORTANT AFTER ALL!

To learn more about the appendix, check out devotion 2 in The Wonder of Creation.

Use the word bank to help Raz fill in the answers to the crossword clues. (Hint: You won't need to use all the words.)

APPENDIX   DIGEST   POUCH   SMALL   STOMACHACHE
BACTERIA   FOOD   PURPOSE   STOMACH

ACROSS

1. The large intestine is attached to the _____ intestine.

2. Scientists once thought the appendix was useless. Now they know it has a very important _____.

3. The appendix stores good _____, which the body needs to break down food.

5. The large intestine, small intestine, and stomach all work together to _____ food.

DOWN

1. The intestines are attached to the _____.

4. The _____ is a little worm-like pouch attached to your large intestine.

> God gave the tiny little appendix an important job to do! You may be young, and you may be small, but God's got important things for you to do too (1 Timothy 4:12)!

FOR YOUR FUNNY BONE

What has a head and a tail but no body?   *A coin*

I sometimes run but I cannot walk. What am I?   *A nose*

Why didn't the skeleton dance?   *Because he had no body to dance with.*

DON'T GIVE UP!

To learn more about the Somali sengis, check out devotion 3 in The Wonder of Creation.

Scientists didn't give up on finding the Somali sengi. No one had seen this little elephant shrew since 1973. But in 2019, with the help of a little peanut butter bait, scientists found them again—in Djibouti, a country in Africa!

Take a look at these two pictures of Adelynn and the Somali sengi. Can you spot all seven differences?

If you ever feel as lost as the Somali sengi, turn to Luke 19:10 for a special promise from God.

MORE THAN A MARBLE

To learn more about the Earth's layers, check out devotion 80 in Indescribable.

Earth might look like a big blue marble floating along in space, but Evyn has learned it's actually made of five different layers. Read about the layers, then label the Earth.

crust: made mostly of granite rock, it ranges from about 3 miles thick under the oceans to over 60 miles thick under mountain ranges

upper mantle: made of both solid and melted rock

lower mantle: made of solid rock that's between 400 and about 1,800 miles below the Earth's surface

outer core: made of melted iron and nickel that creates a magnetic shield so powerful that it reaches into space

inner core: more than 750 miles across and made mostly of super-hot, solid iron

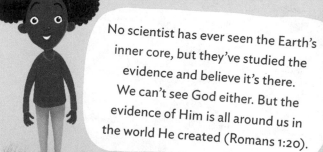

No scientist has ever seen the Earth's inner core, but they've studied the evidence and believe it's there. We can't see God either. But the evidence of Him is all around us in the world He created (Romans 1:20).

_____

_____

_____

_____

_____

PLANET PiZZA!

Make a pizza that shows all the Earth's layers! Use the ingredients below or swap them for your favorites.

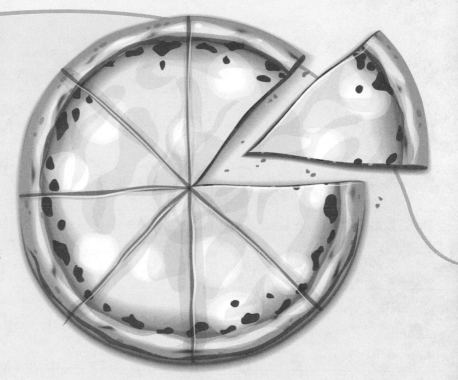

Ingredients

- pizza dough
- jar of pizza sauce
- shredded mozzarella
- chopped bell peppers
- chopped ham
- pepperoni
- cooked sausage crumbles

Tools

- pizza pan
- spoon

Directions

1. Ask a grown-up to help preheat the oven to 450 degrees Fahrenheit.

2. Roll out the pizza dough to fit your pizza pan.

3. Use a spoon to spread the sauce almost—but not quite—to the edge of the crust. Cover the sauce with cheese.

4. In the center, make a small circle of bell peppers.

5. Place a ring of ham around the bell peppers and then a ring of pepperoni around the ham. Finally, make a ring of sausage around the pepperoni, almost to the edge—leave a little crust showing.

6. With a grown-up's help, bake for 8 to 11 minutes or until the crust is golden brown.

7. Let it set for 5 minutes before slicing.

The bell peppers represent the Earth's *inner core*. The ham is the *outer core*. The pepperoni is the *lower mantle*. The sausage is the *upper mantle*. And the pizza crust is, well, the *crust*!

WHAT'S THE WEATHER?

Weather is what's happening in the sky and air outside. Scientists are still busy studying it, but God knows all about it. After all, He created it (Jeremiah 10:12–13)!

Check out the weather words below. Then search through the letters to find them all.

```
P S R H S S M E E O
I G A T G O F S N E
H P I M E E L T A Y
N W N A F E I C C S
D R A Z Z I L B I C
F R X W R L V S R E
I J E W O N I T R K
Q G N E H N R A U T
G A S I Q N S I H P
W E J R A P I H U S
```

blizzard: a snowstorm with winds of at least 35 miles an hour

fog: a cloud near the ground

hail: lumps of ice that form in clouds

hurricane: a massive, swirling storm with winds up to 150 miles per hour

rain: water droplets that fall to the ground

sleet: water droplets that freeze before they hit the ground

snow: water vapor that turns to ice crystals and falls to the ground

THIS WAY!

To learn more about fog, check out devotion 73 in Indescribable.

Fog is actually a *stratus* (STRAT-uhs) cloud flying low to the ground. It can be especially dangerous for sailors because it hides rocks close to shore. Sailors depend on light from lighthouses to guide them.

Follow the numbers and connect the dots so this lighthouse can shine!

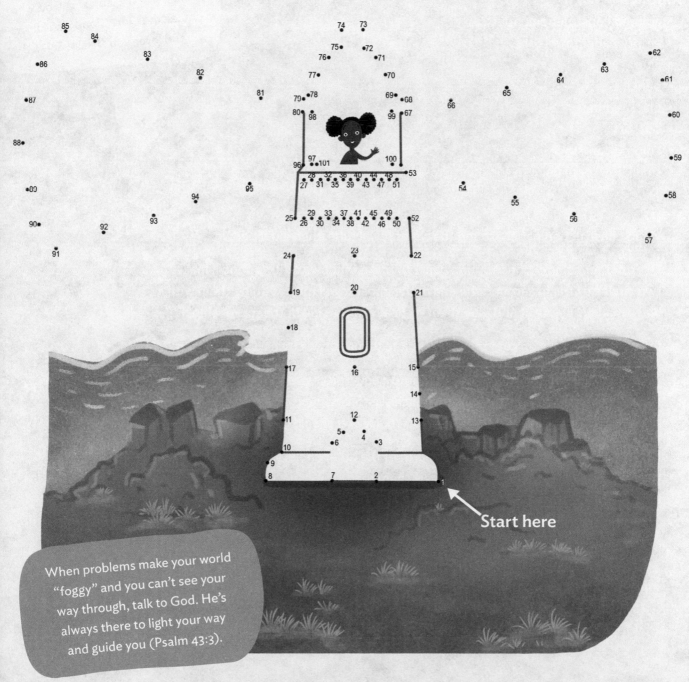

Start here

When problems make your world "foggy" and you can't see your way through, talk to God. He's always there to light your way and guide you (Psalm 43:3).

EXPLORING THE UNKNOWN

To learn more about the Oort Cloud, check out devotion 49 in The Wonder of Creation.

The *Oort (OR-t) Cloud* is a massive ring made up of bits of ice and space debris that surrounds our solar system. The Voyager 1 spacecraft is headed there to find out more, but it won't get there for another 300 years!

If you're traveling out to the Oort Cloud, you'll need a rocket ship. With a grown-up's help, follow the instructions along with Norah to make your own!

> Voyager 1 will spend about 30,000 years traveling *through* the Oort Cloud. Just imagine: the great, big, amazing God who made the Oort Cloud also knows and loves you (Psalm 8:3–6)!

Supplies

- colored construction paper
- empty paper towel tube
- glue
- pencil
- black marker
- scissors
- colored cardstock
- small bowl or plate, 4 to 5 inches across

Steps

1. Wrap construction paper around the paper towel tube, then glue it down.

2. Use another color of construction paper to make windows. With a pencil, make two circles by tracing around the end of the paper towel tube. Outline them with a black marker. Then cut and glue them vertically to the side of the rocket ship.

3. On cardstock, trace around the bowl or plate to make two circles. Cut them out.

4. To make the rocket's stand, cut one circle into 4 equal pieces, as shown. In the bottom of the rocket tube, cut four 1-inch slits. Space them out evenly. Slide a straight side of a circle piece into each slit. Your rocket should now stand up.

5. For the rocket's cone, cut away one-fourth of the other circle, as shown. Bring the two straight edges together and glue them to make a cone. Glue to the top of the rocket.

6. You're ready for takeoff!

Step 4

Step 5

SHINE LiKE JESUS!

To learn more about the Moon, check out devotion 26 in Indescribable.

When Evyn looks into the night sky, she sees the Moon shining bright. Or . . . does she? Actually, the Moon isn't shining! It's reflecting the Sun's light—like a big rocky mirror out in space.

Even though the Moon doesn't create its own light, it still lights up the darkness. We can light up the darkness too! Whenever we're kind, helpful, and loving the way Jesus was, we shine His light into this dark world (Philippians 2:12–15).

Have you seen someone shine with Jesus' light? When have you reflected His light? Use the ideas below—or create your own—to write about those "shining" times.

- I saw my friend shine with the light of Jesus when . . .

- My parent shines like Jesus when . . .

- Today, I can shine by . . .

_____

_____

_____

_____

_____

_____

BiG CHANGES!

To learn more about metamorphosis, check out devotion 100 in Indescribable.

Butterflies aren't born looking like butterflies. Instead, they must go through some pretty big changes—called *metamorphosis* (met-uh-MOHR-fuh-sis)—before they're ready to fly!

Step 1: Egg
An adult butterfly lays an egg on a plant.

Step 2: Caterpillar
The egg hatches, and out crawls a baby caterpillar, also called a *larva* (LAHR-vuh). It begins eating the plant. As the caterpillar grows, it *molts*—or sheds—its skin. It might molt four to five times in this stage.

Step 3: *Pupa* (PYOO-puh)
During the pupa stage, a *chrysalis* (KRIS-uh-lis) forms around the caterpillar like a hard shell. Inside, the wings and antennae are growing. This stage could last from just a few days to over a year, depending on the butterfly species.

Step 4: Butterfly
The butterfly squeezes out of the chrysalis. After its wings dry, the butterfly is ready to fly!

Now draw butterflies in the space below.

A NOT-SO-TASTY SNACK

To learn more about monarch butterflies, check out devotion 21 in How Great Is Our God.

Find out more about butterflies by using the words from the word bank to fill in the blanks below. (Hint: You won't need to use all the words.)

ATTACK	LIZARDS	ORANGE	PURPLE
CATERPILLARS	MILKWEED	POISONOUS	SICK
DEFEND	MONARCH	PREDATOR	SNACK

God gives many of His creations a way to defend themselves against

predators. For example, the _____ butterfly is best known for its
                                1

bright _____ and black wings. But did you know this butterfly is
        2

_____? The poison comes from the _____ plant.
        3   4

Adult monarchs lay their eggs on this poisonous plant.

The eggs hatch into _____, which eat the
                        5

plant. The poison then becomes part of their bodies, and

it stays with them even after they turn into butterflies.

So any _____—like a bird or lizard—
            6

looking for a colorful snack gets a nasty surprise!

HiDE AND SEEK!

To learn more about animals that hide, check out devotion 79 in How Great Is Our God.

God gave the *pygmy* (PIG-me) seahorse a way to stay safe from its enemies: *camouflage* (KAM-uh-flaaj)! This tiny seahorse has the same bumps and coloring as the coral it lives in, making it almost impossible to see.

Lots of sea creatures are hiding in this picture with Evyn. Look closely! Can you find them all?

COULD THAT BE TRUE?

To learn more about the Sun, check out devotion 15 in Indescribable.

God is so big and powerful that He breathed the Sun out of His mouth! (Check out Psalm 33:6.) Test your knowledge of just how big and powerful the Sun is by writing *T* next to each true statement and *F* next to each false one.

_____ 1. The temperature of the Sun's core—or center—is about 27 million degrees Fahrenheit.

_____ 2. The Sun is 93 miles away.

_____ 3. Almost 1 million Earths would fit inside the Sun. That's like filling a school bus with golf balls!

_____ 4. If you get up early enough, you can see the Sun's smiley face.

_____ 5. The Sun is actually a star.

JOKES AND RIDDLES

What does the sun drink out of?	*Sunglasses*
What did the Moon say to the Sun after dinner?	*I'm so full!*
Why did the Sun go to school?	*To get brighter!*
I can be seen where there's light, but when sunlight falls on me, I disappear. What am I?	*A shadow*

ALL MiXED UP!

To learn more about the platypus, check out devotion 67 in The Wonder of Creation.

Want to see God's imagination at work? Check out the platypus! It has the bill of a duck, the body of an otter, and a tail like a beaver. It also has fur *and* webbed feet!

This platypus picture has gotten all mixed up. Can you put the picture back together again? Copy one square of the picture at a time into the empty squares. Use the numbers to guide you.

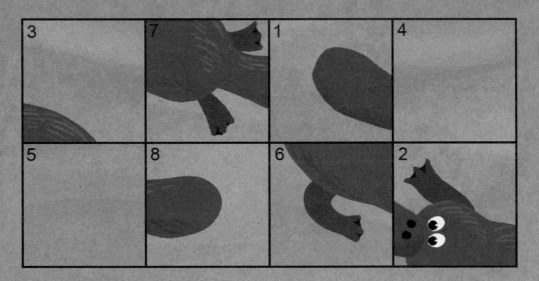

1	2	3	4
5	6	7	8

CRAZY COMBINATIONS!

To learn more about firenados, check out devotion 4 in The Wonder of Creation.

Some combinations are great—like french fries and ketchup. Others are crazy—like fire and a tornado! But that's what happens in some wildfires. As hot, dry air from the wildfire rises, it sometimes starts to spin and pick up fire, creating a *firenado*!

Fill in the blanks below to create your own crazy combinations. Then pick one of those creations and draw it in the space below.

1. Fire + Tornado = Firenado

2. Snow + Rainbow = Snowbow

3. Thunder + _____ = _____

4. _____ + Fog = _____

5. _____ + _____ = _____

Some days feel as bad as a firenado. No matter what's swirling around you, remember that God is always there to help you through it! Just check out His promise in Isaiah 43:5.

DO YOU REMEMBER?

To learn more about memory, check out devotion 54 in The Wonder of Creation.

Short-term memories are remembered only for a little while. They're stored in the brain's frontal lobe. Long-term memories are formed in the *hippocampus* (hip-uh-KAM-puhs). They're usually the memories that matter most!

How's your memory? Grab a timer and set it for 60 seconds. Next, look closely at all the stuff on Raz's shelves. When the timer dings, cover the picture with a piece of paper. How many of these questions you can answer?

1. Name two colors of the books on the short-term memory shelf.

   _____

2. What country is on the map Raz is holding?

   _____

3. What color is the bicycle on Raz's long-term memory shelf?

   _____

4. What kind of hat is on the bottom shelf of Raz's long-term memory?

   _____

5. How many lollipops are on the short-term shelf?

   _____

6. What color shirt is Raz wearing?

   _____

7. What stuffed animal is in Raz's short-term memory?

   _____

8. What kind of ball is in Raz's long-term memory?

   _____

9. Name one of the items on the bottom shelf of Raz's long-term memory.

   _____

10. What is the answer to the math problem in Raz's short-term memory?

   _____

LiKE GLUE!

To learn more about laminin, check out devotion 6 in Indescribable.

Your body is made up of about 37.2 trillion cells. Give or take a million or two. And those cells need to stick together—so God created *laminin* (LAM-uh-nin) to "glue" them all together.

The Bible says that in Jesus "all things hold together" (Colossians 1:17 NIV)—our bodies, our souls, everything! Kind of like laminin. Just take a peek at laminin through a super-powerful microscope, and you'll see an amazing picture of how Jesus holds everything together.

Use the color code to color in the spaces below and discover laminin's amazing shape!

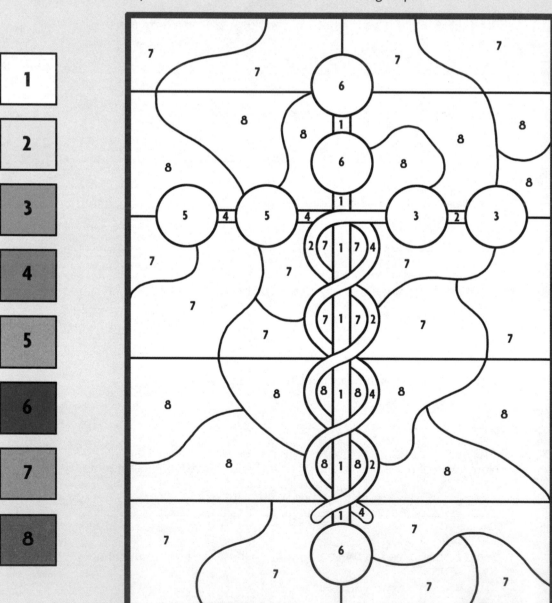

BE A WEATHER WATCHER!

To learn more about clouds, check out devotion 89 in How Great Is Our God.

Clouds come in all shapes, colors, and sizes. And all those different shapes, colors, and sizes give us clues about what the weather will be. Check out these different types of clouds:

 **cirrus** (SIR-uhs): wispy, white clouds that appear high in the sky. They appear in good weather, but they often mean the weather is about to change.

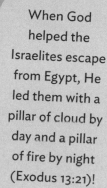 When God helped the Israelites escape from Egypt, He led them with a pillar of cloud by day and a pillar of fire by night (Exodus 13:21)!

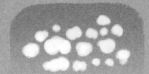 **cirrocumulus** (sir-oh-KYOO-myuh-luhs): small, white clouds high in the sky that look like rows of cotton balls. They appear most often in cold, clear weather.

 **stratus** (STRAT-uhs): thick, low, gray clouds that can cover the whole sky. They mean rain or snow is on the way.

 **cumulus** (KYOO-myuh-luhs): puffy, white clouds that appear on clear, sunny days. They mean good weather is here.

 **cumulonimbus** (kyoo-myuh-loh-NIM-bus): tall clouds that stretch from low in the sky to high. They often mean thunderstorms are on the way.

For the next 5 days, keep a watch on the weather. Use the descriptions above to figure out what kind of clouds you see. Then record the weather that happens with each kind of cloud you observe!

Day	Type of Cloud	Time of Day	Temperature	Colors of Clouds & Sky	Is It Windy?	Is It Raining or Snowing?
Day 1						
Day 2						
Day 3						
Day 4						
Day 5						

PERFECTLY PLANTED

To learn more about plants, check out devotion 84 in Indescribable.

Plants can get the sunlight, water, air, and nutrients they need in some pretty creative ways. For example, God gave desert plants extra-long roots to "dig" deep for water. "Drip tips" help rainforest plants get rid of extra water. And air plants, or *epiphytes* (EP-uh-fites), get their nutrients right from the air!

Every word in this list is connected to plants and how they grow.
Search through the letters below to find them all.

```
A Y V V F D E S E R T N Q S A
R E Z P Q X U Y R A L V T T B
H P M Q X N E E E X E F L N Z
N E Q J L A E M D J A L L E C
T G M I S D J H M Q V O B I K
Z X G R E T A W R R E V F R P
P H U B F F Q Z A O S A A T D
T J E P T A H I S A O D V U N
W I T R L Q N P Q M R T W N E
N Q I S Y F Z C G O J F S A X
K D C U O S E T Y H P I P E F
Y W B R J U G Y V B R A G X K
C Z E G V I A R O Y C B N M A
J S Z Q I H D I I L K W B H L
T E L M I W F D B A T Y A M R
```

AIR	DIRT	LEAVES	RAINFOREST	SUNLIGHT
DESERT	EPIPHYTES	NUTRIENTS	ROOTS	WATER

IN HiS HANDS

To learn more about the Pleiades, check out devotion 42 in Indescribable.

God is so big that He can even hold the *Pleiades* (PLEE-uh-deez) in His hands! *What's that?* The Pleiades are a cluster of over 3,000 stars that stretch some 13 light-years across—that's about 76 trillion miles!

You might not be able to hold 3,000 stars in your hand, but how many marshmallows can you hold? Challenge a friend and see who can hold the most marshmallows in one hand.

Supplies

- paper plate
- bag of miniature marshmallows
- a friend (or a few!)

Steps

1. Pour out the marshmallows onto the plate.

2. Each person should tuck one hand behind their back. Then take turns to see who can grab the most marshmallows in 10 seconds. But wait—you can only pick up one marshmallow at a time!

3. What's the record?

Try this experiment with other objects, like coins, gummy bears, or even socks!

TRY THIS!

- The Pleiades cluster has over 3,000 stars. How many stars can you count in the sky?

- Imagine you discovered a new star. What would you name it?

- What's the biggest ball you can pick up with just one hand? Baseball? Soccer ball? Basketball?

- How fast can you move? Set a timer for 60 seconds and see how many things you can put away in your room.

- With a parent's permission, create an indoor obstacle course with couch cushions, pots and pans, blankets, and other objects. Challenge family and friends to see who can get through it the fastest.

THE SCIENTIFIC METHOD

When scientific thinkers want to know how, when, and why things happen, they use the *scientific method*. By using the scientific method to do tests and experiments, we can learn about the world around us. Here are the steps:

STEP 1: OBSERVATION

See something and wonder about it.

STEP 2: QUESTION

Ask a question about what you observed.

STEP 3: HYPOTHESIS

Form a hypothesis (hi-POTH-us-sis)—
a possible answer—to the question
asked in step 2.

STEP 4: EXPERIMENT

Test the hypothesis.

STEP 5: RECORD

Record the results of the experiment.

STEP 6: CONCLUSION

Study the data and decide if the hypothesis was correct.

LET'S EXPERIMENT!

Have you ever seen people put salt on icy roads and sidewalks? Why do they do that?
Does it make the ice melt faster? Use the scientific method to find out!

Supplies

- 2 small bowls
- ice cubes
- measuring spoons
- salt
- timer

Steps

1. Decide on your hypothesis. It might be something like this: *I believe adding salt will make the ice cubes melt faster.* Or it could be this: *I believe the plain ice will melt faster.* Write your hypothesis in the chart.

2. Fill the two bowls with ice cubes. Use the same number of cubes in each.

3. Sprinkle three tablespoons of salt onto the ice in one of the bowls. Do nothing to the other bowl.

4. Set the timer for 10 minutes.

5. When the timer dings, check the ice. Which has melted more? Record that in the chart.

6. Set the timer for another 10 minutes and check the ice again. Record the results.

7. Set the timer for 10 minutes one last time. Check the ice and record the results.

8. What's your conclusion? Did the ice with or without the salt melt faster? Was your hypothesis correct?

	EXPERIMENT LOG	
Step 1	Observe	People put salt on icy roads and sidewalks.
Step 2	Question	Does salt make the ice melt faster?
Step 3	Hypothesis	
Step 4	Experiment	
Step 5	Record the Data	After 10 minutes: After 20 minutes: After 30 minutes:
Step 6	Conclusion	

HAPPY HOPPING

To learn more about bunnies and their binkies, check out devotion 98 in The Wonder of Creation.

God gave bunnies one of the funniest ways to show their happiness: the binky! When bunnies are happy, they hop, twist, and groove in a move called the *binky*!

Each bunny has their own unique binky style. Map out this bunny's binky moves by following this order:

"Hop" just one square at a time—up, down, or across, but not diagonally—to get to the finish line.

FEELING A LITTLE *HANGRY?*

To learn more about that hangry feeling, check out devotion 93 in The Wonder of Creation.

Joshua is feeling a little hangry. What's that hangry feeling all about? Unscramble the words to find out!

When you combine **gyrnuh** _____ and **gryna** _____, you get a nasty little
1   2

feeling called **hgryna** _____. Hangry is more than just a bad **ttiudaet** _____,
3   4

though. There's actual stuff happening inside your **doyb** _____.
5

Your body uses the food you eat to make simple **rsgasu** _____. It then uses those sugars
6

for **grynee** _____. When you haven't eaten and you're running low on energy, your brain thinks
7

you're in **lbetoru** _____. It sends out the **igfth** _____-or-**lfihgt** _____
8   9   10

chemical called *adrenaline* (uh-DREN-uh-lin)—and you get hangry! Being hangry makes it harder to

lrtcnoo _____ your emotions, and you get upset about things that don't usually bother you.
11

What's the cure? Eat something!

When you're hangry, you might say or do things you later wish you hadn't. Grab a snack, take a deep breath, and say you're sorry to the person you hurt—and to God. He promises to forgive you (1 John 1:9).

rumble grumble!

WOULD YOU RATHER?

Would you rather eat a raw potato or an entire lemon?
Would you rather give up sweets or video games for a year?
Would you rather eat an ant or be stung by a bee?
Would you rather eat only your favorite food for the rest of your
    life or never eat your favorite food again?
Would you rather drink ketchup with a straw or eat mustard with a spoon?

GOD MADE YOU AMAZING!

To learn more about the Whirlpool Galaxy, check out devotion 55 in Indescribable.

Zoom off into space about 31 million light-years away, and you'll find the Whirlpool Galaxy. It's one of the places where God creates stars.

Even more amazing than the way God makes stars is the way He knit you together (Psalm 139:13–14). Each detail is carefully planned, right down to the gifts He put inside of you. These aren't like birthday gifts—they're even cooler! They're things like serving, teaching, and encouraging (Romans 12:6–8).

Take this quiz to learn more about the gifts God has put inside you. Next to each statement, write the number that best fits you. Add up the numbers in each section. The sections with the highest scores are where your gifts might be.

> **1**—Not me   **2**—Sometimes me   **3**—That's always me!

Serving

_____ I look for ways to help others.

_____ I love helping others take out the trash, rake leaves, or wash dishes.

_____ When people ask me to help, I usually say yes.

_____ *Total*

Teaching

_____ I love helping people learn about the Bible.

_____ I love learning new facts.

_____ I enjoy coming up with puppet shows, songs, and other ways to tell Bible stories.

_____ *Total*

Encouraging

_____ I notice when others are good at something, and I tell them how good they are.

_____ I have a positive outlook and like to focus on the good things in life.

_____ I love listening to what others have to say.

_____ *Total*

Giving

_____I think it's fun to give money and gifts to others.

_____I like making gifts for others.

_____I think about ways I can give to people who need help.

_____*Total*

Leading

_____I enjoy organizing activities.

_____I always want to do my best.

_____I usually take charge in a group.

_____*Total*

Kindness and Compassion

_____I love helping others fix their problems.

_____I enjoy making others smile.

_____When others are hurting, I feel sad too.

_____*Total*

What gifts do you see inside you?

_____

_____

_____

SMILE!

To learn more about teeth, check out devotion 75 in The Wonder of Creation.

Reading the Bible every day will keep your faith strong. But what about your teeth? What keeps them strong? Brushing and flossing them each day!

Answer these questions to fill in the crossword puzzle with some "toothy" facts.

ACROSS

3. This kind of doctor helps take care of your teeth.
6. When you get a hole in your tooth from decay, it's called this.
7. What do you say when you smile for the camera?
8. The front teeth, or *incisors* (in-SI-zurz), are good for this.
10. You should brush and _____ every day.

DOWN

1. Back teeth, or *molars* (MOH-lerz), are for _____ food. (Hint: It rhymes with *finding*.)
2. What do you put on your toothbrush?
4. Your teeth are covered in this pearly white, super-hard stuff.
5. Close your mouth when you _____ your food!
8. Enamel is the hardest thing in your body. It's even harder than your _____.
9. This is what your mouth does when you're happy.

HAPPY NAPPING

To learn more about napping, check out devotion 97 in The Wonder of Creation.

NASA did a study on napping and discovered that astronauts were happier, more creative, and more alert after a short nap.

Some animals appreciate a little extra snoozing time too. Dogs doze away about half the day, and cats are famous for their naps. (Catnap, anyone?) Dolphins sleep with one eye open to keep a watch out for danger. Otters float in the water for their naps, holding on to seaweed—or other otters—to keep from drifting away. And *frigate* (FRIH-guht) birds even nap as they fly along on their months-long journey across the ocean!

KNOW YOUR NAP FACTS

1. What did NASA learn about naps?

   _____

2. What kind of bird naps as it flies?

   _____

3. What animal sleeps with one eye open?

   _____

4. How much of a day do dogs sleep?

   _____

5. How do otters keep from drifting away as they doze?

   _____

You might not want to nap in the water or midair, but you can rest anywhere knowing that God never sleeps. He's always awake and always watching over you (Psalm 121:4)!

THE PERFECT ZZZS

The Indescribable gang enjoys a good nap! Try these tips for your own perfect nap:

- Nap before 3:00 p.m. so that it doesn't mess up your nighttime sleep.
- Pick a good spot—one that's dark and quiet.
- Snuggle up with a favorite blanket, pillow, or stuffed pal.
- Don't sleep too long or it can be hard to wake up. Ten to 20 minutes is about right.

CLUES iN THE ROCK

To learn more about fossils, check out devotion 65 in Indescribable.

Some rocks are *fossils*—rocks with the imprints of ancient animals or plants left in them.

Fossils can form when an animal dies, especially if its body sinks into mud. Over time, *sedimentary* (seh-duh-MEN-tuh-ree) rocks—small bits of rocks, shells, or bones cemented together—form around the animal's remains and create a fossil.

Scientists called *paleontologists* (pay-lee-on-TALL-uh-jists) study fossils to learn about long-ago plants and animals. Imagine you're a paleontologist headed to a dig site. Follow the instructions and the map to figure out your journey across the island to the site. Draw your path from the rowboat to the fossil!

1. Jump in the rowboat and paddle over to the supply tent. Circle seven supplies you'll need. Do you want the soft paintbrush, glasses, hat, pickax, magnifying glass, water bottle, binoculars, book about fossils, sunscreen, or shovel?

2. Load everything into your backpack. Now you're ready to cross the stream. How will you get across without getting wet?

    _____

3. Hike through the forest. How many trees are in the forest?

    _____

4. How will you get down the cliff to the dig site?

    _____

5. Your backpack is too heavy! Which two supplies will you leave behind?

    _____

6. Now head to the dig site. It looks like it's in the middle of a desert. Which supply item do you need to stay hydrated?

    _____

    If you don't have it with you, travel back to the tent and switch one of your supplies for it.

7. The team has already found one fossil! Look at those short arms, that long tail, and those big teeth. What could this fossil be?

    _____

8. What tool could you use to finish cleaning away the dirt from the skeleton? Remember, you'll need to be extra careful!

_____

If you don't have this supply with you, start over and try again!

IT'S *ELEMENTARY!*

When God made the world, He used ingredients called *elements*, like carbon, oxygen, and gold. Elements have only one kind of atom—they're the most basic substances in our world. But they combine to make everything else! For example, two hydrogens combined with one oxygen make the *compound* we call water, or H_2O.

There are 118 elements, and they're arranged in the *periodic table of elements*. Each square holds a lot of information: the element's name, symbol, and atomic number.

In this periodic table, some of the names are missing. Follow the clues to fill in the answers.

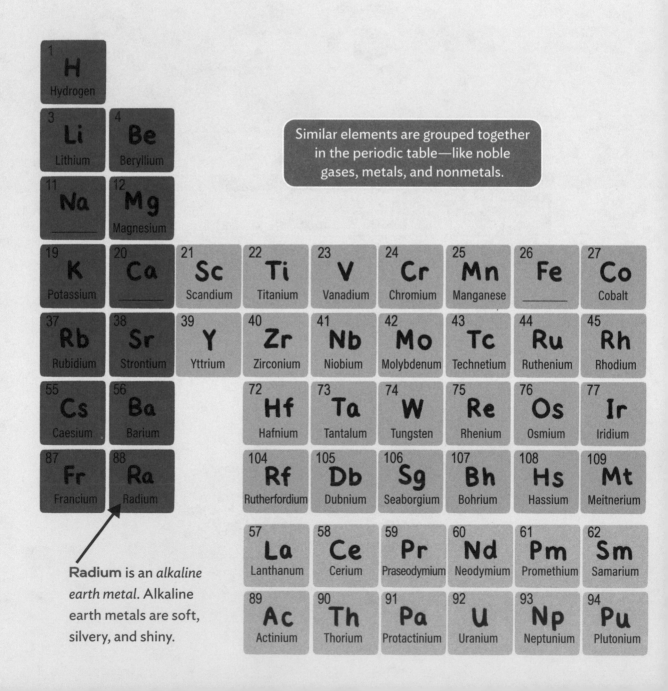

Similar elements are grouped together in the periodic table—like noble gases, metals, and nonmetals.

Radium is an *alkaline earth metal*. Alkaline earth metals are soft, silvery, and shiny.

ATOMIC NUMBER	CLUES	ANSWERS
2	Balloons float when they're filled with this element.	_____
8	This element is in the air we breathe.	_____
11	This element tastes salty.	_____
20	This element makes teeth and bones strong.	_____
26	If you lift weights, you might get to be as strong as this heavy metal.	_____
28	A coin worth five cents shares a name with this element.	_____
47	At Christmas, carolers sing a song about bells made of this metal.	_____
79	This shiny yellow metal element is often used to make coins and jewelry.	_____

Lead is a *post-transition metal*. These metals are good conductors of heat and electricity.

Copper is a *transition metal*. Our bodies need some of these metals, like iron, zinc, and chromium, to stay healthy.

Argon is a *noble gas*. Noble gases are colorless and odorless.

Sulfur is a *nonmetal*. Nonmetals are found in the Earth's crust, in the atmosphere, and even in your body.

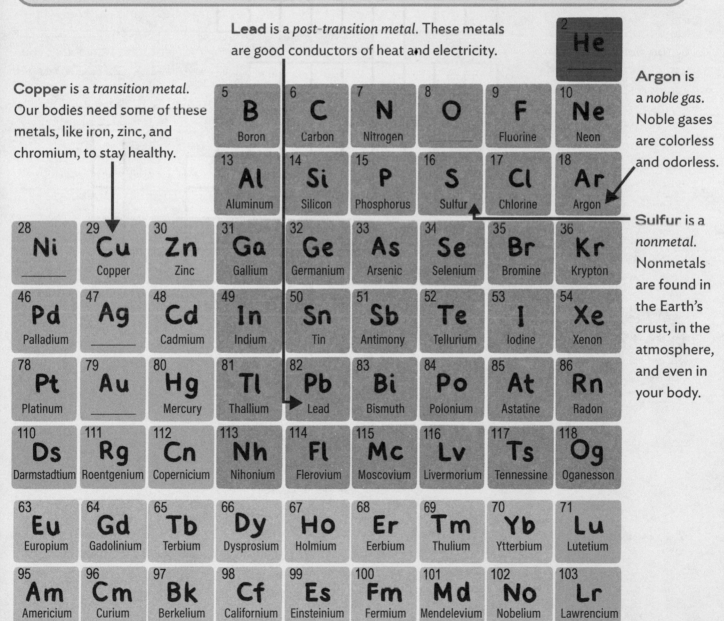

BLESS YOU!

To learn more about germs, check out devotion 18 in The Wonder of Creation.

Sharing makes God smile. But Clarke is sharing one thing we never want to share: germs! (Sneeze into your elbow, Clarke!) Use the word bank to fill in the answers to the crossword clues to explore more about these microscopic invaders. (Hint: You won't need to use all the words.)

DOWN

1. A _____ can be a virus, bacteria, parasite, or fungus.
2. You can get rid of a lot of germs by _____ your hands.
6. You should cough into your _____ so that you don't share your germs.
7. When you cough or sneeze into the air, tiny _____ drops fly everywhere.
8. Germs try to invade your body and make you _____.
10. You might _____ when you have a cold.

ACROSS

3. Germs are tiny living _____.
4. The scientific name for a germ is _____.
5. We often say, "Bless you!" when someone _____.
9. Germs are so tiny that you need a _____ to see them.

Word Bank:

BURP	ELBOW	INVADE	PATHOGEN	WASHING
COUGH	GERM	MICROSCOPE	SICK	WATER
COVER	HOURS	ORGANISMS	SNEEZES	

RiGHT iN THE EYE!

To learn more about the Eye of the Sahara, check out devotion 94 in The Wonder of Creation.

Finish writing the story below and tell what happens next!

Dear Travel Diary,

Earlier today, Joshua and I were soaring over the mysterious Eye of the Sahara in our hot-air balloon. It stared up at us like a gigantic, unblinking eyeball—a 25-mile-wide, bright blue eyeball! Then I heard a terrible ripping sound. A bird had flown straight into our balloon, and its beak tore a gigantic hole in it! Suddenly we were dropping—fast! We were going to crash right in the middle of that bright blue eye . . .

JUST A *LITTLE* DIFFERENT

To learn more about the names of baby animals, check out devotion 14 in Indescribable.

A baby cat is a *kitten*, and a baby dog is a *puppy*. But what about a baby fox? It's a *kit*. And a *duckling* grows up to be a duck, a *fry* becomes a fish, and a *puggle* becomes a platypus!

Take a close look at these groups of baby animals. Circle the animal in each group that's just a *little* different.

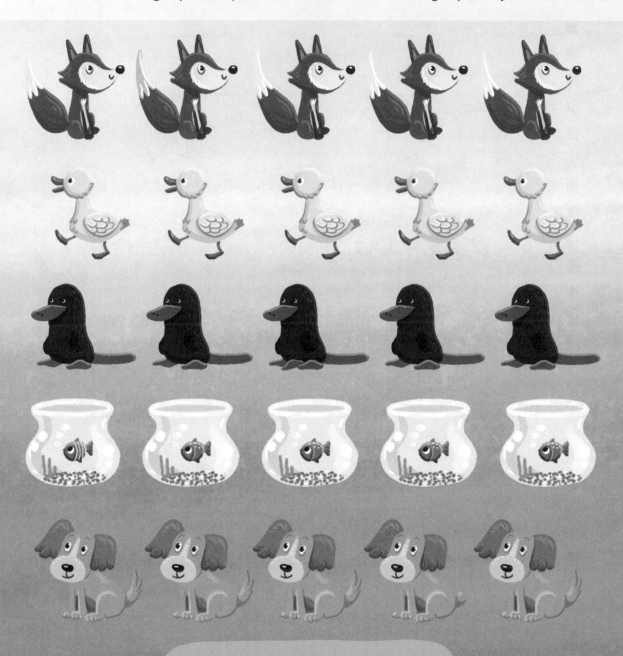

Jesus was once a kid like you. As He grew, His body got taller and stronger. But most importantly, Jesus grew in His knowledge and love of God (Luke 2:52)—and you can too!

CELL-EBRATiON!

To learn more about cells, check out devotion 66 in Indescribable.

Every living thing is made up of one or more cells. They're the building blocks God uses to create life. Most cells are either animal or plant cells. Animal cells (which make up bodies) have three main parts: cell membrane, cytoplasm, and nucleus.

Use the definitions below to help you label the parts of this animal cell.

Cell membrane (MEM-brain): this thin but tough wall surrounding the cell acts like a guard, letting the good things in while keeping the bad stuff out.

Cytoplasm (SI-tuh-pla-zuhm): mostly made of water, it gives the cell its shape and contains *organelles* (OR-guh-nelz) that make proteins and change food into energy.

Nucleus (NOO-klee-uhs): the "brain" of the cell, it tells the cell when to grow and reproduce.

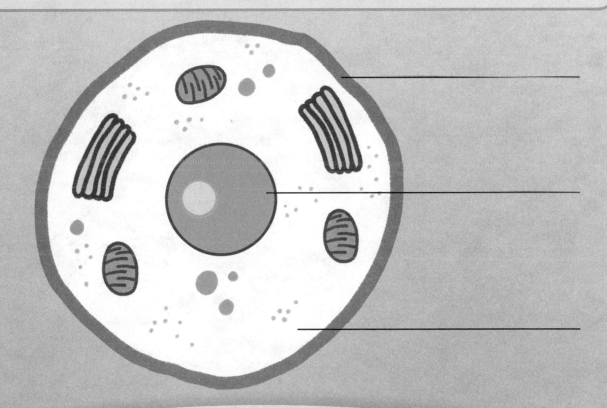

DiD YOU KNOW?

- Plant cells have a tough cell wall around the cell membrane. It helps the plant stand upright.

- Bacteria are living organisms that have only one cell.

- Most cells are tiny—over 10,000 human cells could fit on the head of a pin.

- The largest single cell is the yolk of an ostrich egg, which can weigh as much as three pounds!

SAY, "CHEESE!"

*To learn more about **Voyager 1**, check out devotion 77 in Indescribable.*

Imagine seeing God's creation from space! That's what Voyager 1 helped us do. In 1977, NASA launched it on a picture-taking mission. Thirteen years later, after rocketing past Pluto, Voyager 1 turned around and took a picture of Earth. It's called the Pale Blue Dot photo—because Earth looked like a tiny dot in space.

Draw a line to help Voyager 1 get from Earth to the camera spot as fast as you can.
Stay between the lines and don't "crash" into any planets along the way!

WHEREVER YOU GO

To learn more about turtle shells, check out devotion 27 in The Wonder of Creation.

Use the words from the word bank to help Evyn fill in the blanks and
learn more about turtles and their mobile fortresses!

Imagine carrying your own personal _____ everywhere you go. That's life for
<u>1</u>

_____ and tortoises. From the 1,500-pound leatherback turtle to the tiny, three-inch-long
<u>2</u>

Cape tortoise, the one thing they all have in common is their _____.
<u>3</u>

That shell is made up of about 60 _____ and covered with tough plates called
<u>4</u>

_____ (skoots). The shell is attached to their _____ and acts like a rib cage to
<u>5</u> <u>6</u>

protect the turtle's soft body. When threatened, they can pull back into their shells to stay safe.

You've got your own personal fortress too. No, not a big, bony shell on your back. In

fact, your fortress is even tougher than a turtle's shell—it's God. He surrounds you with

His _____ and goes with you wherever you go!
<u>7</u>

BONES   LOVE   SHELL   TURTLES
FORTRESS   SCUTES   SPiNE

What has armor but isn't a knight, snaps but isn't a twig,
and is always at home even when it's on the move?

You guessed it—a turtle! Share this riddle with your
friends and see who comes up with the right answer!

HOW COOL ARE YOU?

To learn more about snowflakes, check out devotion 28 in The Wonder of Creation.

Snowflakes are clear ice crystals that form high in the clouds. When packed together, they look white. If you look closely, you'll find that God never makes two snowflakes exactly alike. Each is beautiful in its own way—like you and me!

Norah caught a snowflake. She and Adelynn decided to give it a name: Snowellapi. How many words can you create using only the letters in Snowellapi? (Examples: *snap, low,* and *sap.*) Write them all here.

_____   _____

_____   _____

_____   _____

_____   _____

_____   _____

_____   _____

_____   _____

How did you do?

0–5: Your brain is feeling a little slushy! Keep looking!

6–10: Pretty cool thinking!

11–15: You're as sharp as an ice crystal!

16–20: You've got a blizzard of smarts!

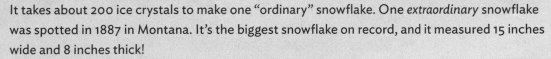

LET IT SNOW!

It takes about 200 ice crystals to make one "ordinary" snowflake. One *extraordinary* snowflake was spotted in 1887 in Montana. It's the biggest snowflake on record, and it measured 15 inches wide and 8 inches thick!

With a grown-up's help, follow these instructions to make your own snowflake.

Supplies

- 4 pipe cleaners (for each snowflake)
- scissors
- fishing line
- wooden spoon
- large glass bowl
- water
- microwave-safe bowl
- borax laundry soap
- spoon
- plate

Steps

1. Cut 2 pipe cleaners in half. Twist 3 of the halves together to make a star.

2. Cut the remaining half piece in half again. Cut another pipe cleaner into 4 pieces—so that you have 6 pieces—all about the same size.

3. Cut the last pipe cleaner into 6 pieces.

4. Wrap all the pieces around the points of your star to make a pattern—any pattern you want.

5. Cut a piece of fishing line and tie one end to the snowflake. Tie the other end of the line around a wooden spoon.

6. Lay the wooden spoon across a large glass bowl filled with water. Adjust the length of the line so the snowflake is completely in the water but doesn't touch the bowl's bottom.

7. Add 4 cups of water to a separate microwave-safe bowl. Ask a grown-up to help you microwave the water until it is hot but not boiling.

8. Add ⅔ cup of borax to the hot water and stir until dissolved. Slowly pour over your snowflake so that it is covered. (Make more borax solution, if needed.)

9. Let it sit for 1–2 days. Don't move or touch it! The borax will cover your snowflake in crystals!

10. Using the spoon, gently lift the snowflake and place it on a plate to dry. Carefully cut away the fishing line. When it's completely dry, use another piece of fishing line to make a loop for hanging.

11. Hang your snowflake in your window, put it on the refrigerator, or share it with a friend!

BiG, BiGGER, . . . BiGGEST?

To learn more about Betelgeuse, check out devotion 34 in Indescribable.

If you want to get a glimpse of how big and powerful God is, look up at *Betelgeuse* (sounds like "beetle juice"). Betelgeuse is 640 light-years away, but it's so big that you can see it without a telescope. In fact, it's so huge that 262 trillion Earths could fit inside of it.

Imagine you're an astronomer studying the stars, and you've just discovered the biggest star anyone has ever found! Use your creativity to record all the "facts" in the report below.

STAR DISCOVERY REPORT

Date discovered: _____

Astronomer's name: _____

What telescope was used to find the star?

_____

What will the star be named?

_____

How many light-years from Earth is it?

_____

What galaxy is it in?

_____

How large is it?

_____

How many Earths would fit inside of it?

_____

WHO'S BEEN HERE?

To learn more about animal tracks, check out devotion 23 in The Wonder of Creation.

Animals are everywhere! How can you know which animals are sharing the world around you? By the footprints, or tracks, they leave behind. They're especially easy to see in mud, soft dirt, sand, and snow.

Read through the descriptions and draw a line to match each animal to its track.

Squirrel tracks have four toes on the front feet and five on the back. But when they're running, their back feet land first.

Elephant tracks are round and huge—about 23 inches long! You're not likely to see these tracks in your neighborhood!

Bird tracks are usually thin with three toes pointing to the front and one toe pointing backward.

Animals in the **dog** family have four toes on both the front and back feet. The little triangles over the toes are made by their claws.

Thin lines that loop and curl around belong to **earthworms**!

Animals in the **cat** family leave tracks with four toes on the front and back feet. No claws show in their tracks because they tuck them inside their paws.

Two-toed tracks probably belong to an animal in the **deer** family.

Raccoon tracks have five toes on the front and back that look like little handprints.

Jesus asks us to be kind, help others, and love everyone. Why? Because when we do those things, we leave "tracks" for others to follow . . . all the way back to Him (John 13:35)!

AMAZING ANTS

To learn more about ants, check out devotion 19 in The Wonder of Creation.

Everything in God's creation has a purpose—even ants. The queen lays the eggs. Drones take care of the queen. And though worker ants are the smallest, they do all the other work, like caring for baby ants, taking out the trash, finding food, and protecting the nest.

Trace the lines to see which worker ant makes it back to the nest!

A GALAXY OF STARS

To learn more about the Milky Way Galaxy, check out devotion 12 in Indescribable.

The Milky Way is filled with billions of stars—maybe as many as 400 billion or even more! Scientists don't know exactly how many, but God does. He knows everything (Psalm 147:5)!

Color this picture of Clarke as an astronaut exploring a tiny corner of the Milky Way.

SEARCHING CENOTES

To learn more about cenotes, check out devotion 14 in How Great Is Our God.

A *cenote* (sih-NOH-tee) is a sinkhole that forms when the ceiling of an underground cave, well, *caves* in and the hole is filled with water. The Yucatán Peninsula of Mexico has thousands of cenotes. Archaeologists exploring these pools have found fossils of mammoths, sloths, and camels! What might Adelynn and Raz find?

Search through the letters below to find these words about the Yucatán Peninsula cenotes:

CAVE

DIVE

FOSSIL

MAMMOTH

SINKHOLE

STALACTITES

STALAGMITES

UNDERGROUND

WATER

```
O D Z S W U A S W R K F
N S N I C A V E A H P D
A I E U L N Z C T C Z E
Y O U T O G T O E E C G
I R E J I R M L R N Z I
U F R I R M G R S T Q Q
P P C T A E G R B E N I
E X R M J E V A E R S K
T C U F O S S I L D R T
S I N K H O L E D A N T
V A T X D F C M D Y T U
S S E T I T C A L A T S
```

When you search for God, He promises you will always find Him! And you can find that promise in Jeremiah 29:13.

ON THE LOOKOUT!

To learn more about desert life, check out devotion 71 in How Great Is Our God.

God made sure animals in the desert can find water—sometimes in unusual ways! Like the *peccary* (PEH-kuh-ree), a pig-like animal. God gave it an extra-tough mouth and tummy so it can chow down on water-rich cactuses, prickly spines and all!

A lot of desert creatures are hiding in the picture below. Look closely! Can you find them all?

| BAT | FOX | LIZARD | PECCARY | SNAKE |
| CAMEL | FROG | OWL | SCORPION | TORTOISE |

NOW THAT'S HOT!

To learn more about lava, check out devotion 91 in How Great Is Our God.

Lava is melted rock that gets as hot as 2,200 degrees Fahrenheit. When it's underground, that melted rock is called *magma*. But when it spews out of a volcano or creeps up through cracks in the Earth's surface, its name changes to *lava*. Skate fast, Evyn!

See how "hot" your lava knowledge is. Write *T* next to each true statement and *F* next to each false one.

_____ 1. The Hawaiian Islands were formed by underwater lava piling higher and higher.

_____ 2. Lava comes from melted soil.

_____ 3. Melted rock that creeps up through cracks in the Earth's surface is called *magma*.

_____ 4. Lava can move as fast as 35 miles per hour.

When you get angry, don't let your words spew out like lava! Stop and ask God to control your words (Psalm 141:3).

VOLCANO!

To learn more about volcanoes, check out devotion 20 in The Wonder of Creation.

Volcanoes are openings in the crust of the Earth that lead down to pools of *magma*, or super-hot, melted rock. Help Adelynn label the parts of this volcano and discover facts about each part.

An **ash cloud** forms when underground water is heated by the magma and changes to steam. As the steam rushes to escape into the air, it picks up tiny bits of rock, minerals, and volcanic glass, forming the cloud over the volcano.

The **crater** is the mouth of the volcano.

Lava is the melted rock that flows out of the volcano.

A **side vent** is an opening in the side of the volcano where lava and gases can escape.

The **magma chamber** is a large pool of melted rock deep under the crust of the Earth.

Layers of lava and ash cool and settle, forming rock layers. Those rock layers can build up into mountains and even islands.

REACH FOR THE STARS!

To learn more about stars, check out devotion 31 in Indescribable.

Stars don't live forever. Smaller stars simply shrink away. But larger stars die in a massive explosion of color and light called a *supernova*. To find out more about stars, help Evyn fill in the answers to the crossword clues.

ACROSS

2. Out on the sea, _____ use stars to help navigate their ships.
5. Stars are basically gigantic balls of _____.
6. Stars are far away in outer _____.
7. There's a song that tells a little star to _____, but stars don't really do this.
8. A star is held together by _____. (It also keeps your feet on the ground.)
10. The Earth orbits around this star.

DOWN

1. A supernova sometimes leaves behind a _____ hole. (It's the opposite of white.)
2. A _____ is the biggest explosion humans have ever seen!
3. The wise men followed one to find Jesus.
4. Some people like to make a _____ on the first star they see at night.
8. _____ created the stars.
9. Stars can live for billions of _____.

Stars might not live forever, but you can live forever with Jesus when you choose to love and follow Him (John 3:16).

WAY UNDER THE WAVES

To learn more about ocean fish, check out devotion 5 in Indescribable.

Deep in the ocean, scientists are discovering the strangest creatures! Like the 5,000-pound giant sunfish that weighs more than an SUV! And then there's the fangtooth fish. Its needle-sharp fangs are so long, it can't close its mouth!

Raz went exploring underwater, but his picture has been sliced to ribbons! Can you put it back in order again? Write the letter of each piece in the correct order in the blanks below. What word do the letters spell? (Hint: If you get stuck, cut out the pieces and then put the puzzle in the correct order. But make sure you complete the activity on page 124 first!)

D I _ _ _ _ _ _ _

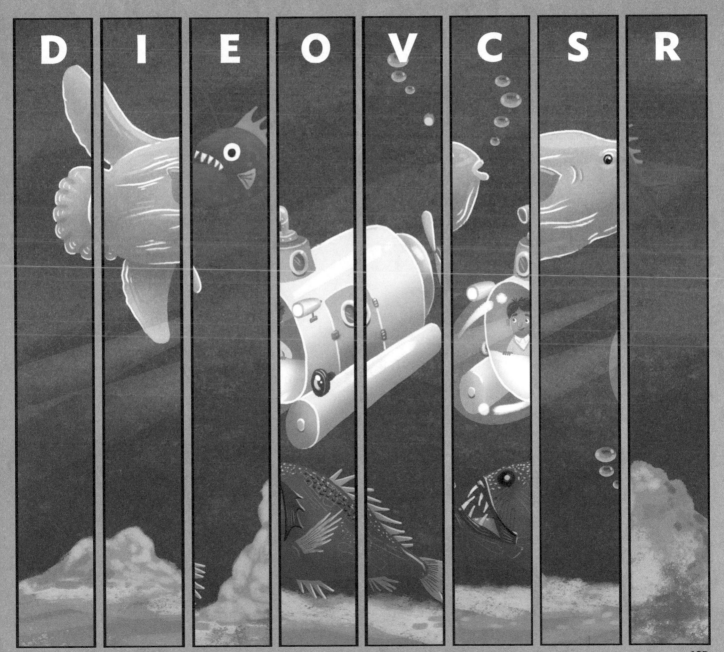

God created a butterfly's wings with a plan and a purpose. The darker colors soak up the sunlight and help the cold-blooded butterfly warm up enough to fly. And brightly colored patterns warn predators away, saying, "Don't eat me! I taste *really* bad."

Connect the dots to see who's fluttering through the flowers, then color in your own bright colors and patterns.

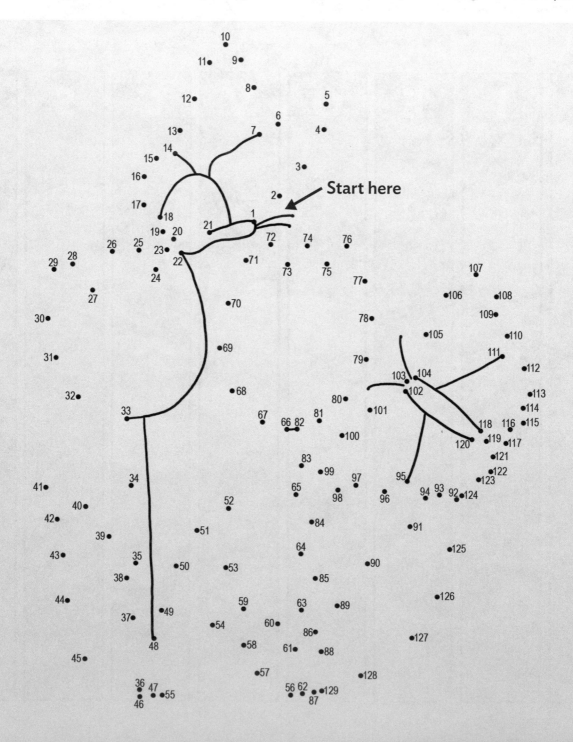

WALKING WATER EXPERIMENT

Plants soak up water and other nutrients through their roots in a process called *capillary* (KAP-uh-ler-ee) *action*. That's when a liquid moves up something solid, like a tube (or plant stem).

Try this experiment and watch the water "walk" from one glass to the next using capillary action.

Supplies

- 7 clear glasses or cups
- paper and pen
- water
- red, yellow, and blue food coloring
- spoon
- paper towels

Steps

1. Ask a grown-up to help you find 7 glasses and line them up in a row. Use the paper and pen to make labels and number each glass from 1 to 7.

2. Fill glasses 1, 3, 5, and 7 with water.

3. Add a few drops of red food coloring to glasses 1 and 7. Add yellow to glass 3. Add blue to glass 5. (Glasses 2, 4, and 6 will be empty.)

4. Stir water with a spoon to mix in the coloring. (Wipe off the spoon between colors.) Add more drops of coloring if you want the water to be darker.

5. Fold a paper towel in half long ways, and then again, and again. Keep folding until the paper towel is a 1-to-2-inch-wide tube. Then fold the tube in half to make a V shape. Repeat this with more paper towels to make six V's.

6. Put one end of a paper towel V in glass 1 and the other end in glass 2. Put the end of another paper towel V in glass 2 and the other end in glass 3. Repeat until all the glasses are connected.

7. Watch what happens over time (20 minutes, 1 hour, 3 hours, and the next day). Record the results in the chart below.

	20 Minutes	1 Hour	3 Hours	Next Day
What happened to the paper towels?				
How much water moved to the "empty" glasses?				
What color is the water in the "empty" glasses?				

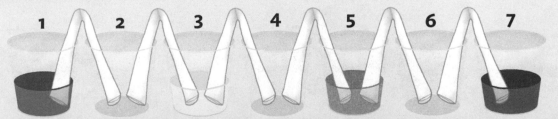

THEY'RE BACK?

To learn more about dinosaurs in the Bible, check out devotion 3 in Indescribable.

In the Bible, the book of Job talks about all kinds of animals, from eagles to lions to dinosaurs. That's right—dinosaurs! Just check out the massive behemoth in Job 40:15–24. Amazing! We don't see dinosaurs roaming around anymore, but what if we did?

Team up with a friend or two for this fill-in-the-blank fun. Don't read the story yet! First, fill in each blank with the type of word listed. Next, add the words to the story, matching the numbered words to the numbered blanks. Then go back and read the whole story to find out what happens when a dinosaur comes for dinner!

1. A friend's name: _____

2. A word ending with -ing: _____

3. Animal (plural): _____

4. Body part (plural): _____

5. Adjective: _____

6. Kind of dinosaur: _____

7. Body part: _____

8. Verb ending in -ed: _____

9. Verb ending in -ed: _____

10. Funny noise ending in -ed: _____

11. Verb ending in -ed: _____

12. Body part: _____

13. A game: _____

14. A way of moving that ends in -ed:

_____

15. Silly name for a pet: _____

16. Something at the playground: _____

17. Verb ending in -ed: _____

18. Food (plural): _____

19. Drink: _____

20. Funny noise ending in -ed: _____

21. A zoo animal: _____

22. A kitchen appliance: _____

My pal _____ and I were playing ball in the park when suddenly . . . *BOOM! Ka-THUD! CRASH!*
1

It sounded like _____ _____! The ground was shaking under our _____. Suddenly,
2   3   4

out of the trees, a _____ dinosaur came running straight at us! It was a real, live _____! I
5   6

was so scared that my _____ _____, and _____ _____!
7   8   1   9

That _____ screeched to a stop right in front of us. It snatched our ball and _____. It
6   10

even _____ its tail. Before I could run away, it dropped the ball right in front of my _____.
11   12

Did this thing want to play _____? I slowly picked up the ball and threw it. The dinosaur
13

_____ after it! We decided to name it _____.
14   15

After a few rounds of catch, we all headed over to the playground. First, _____ jumped on
15

the _____. Then we climbed up on its back and _____.
16   17

When it was time to go home, _____ and I waved goodbye. But _____ followed me
1   15

home!

Grandma was *really* surprised when a _____ sat down to dinner. It gobbled down all the
6

_____ and drank a whole bottle of _____. Then it _____ so loud that my pet
18   19   20

_____ hid under the bed!
21

When _____ had eaten every last crumb and was starting to chew on the _____,
15   22

Grandma said it was time for bed. But the _____ had to sleep in the backyard. That big, tough
6

dinosaur started shaking and whining. It was scared of the dark! So I brought out my _____
21

to help. But when _____ curled up with it and yawned widely, my _____ looked a little
15   21

worried!

127

COUNT ON IT!

To learn more about what can't be counted, check out devotion 50 in Indescribable.

Some things can't be counted—there are just too many of them! Like grains of sand. Researchers estimate that Earth's beaches hold more than 7.5 quintillion grains of sand. And the Bible tells us that God's thoughts outnumber even the grains of sand (Psalm 139:17–18)!

Test your memory and counting skills. Grab a timer and set it for 60 seconds. Next, take a close look at this busy picture. When the timer dings, cover the picture with a piece of paper. Then see how many of the questions on the next page you can answer!

1. How many stars are on the blue flag?

_____

2. What color is Norah's beach towel?

_____

3. How many crabs are creeping across the sand?

_____

4. How many pails are there?

_____

5. List three colors of shovels.

_____

6. How many birds are on the sand?

_____

7. How many birds are flying through the air?

_____

8. What is Evyn holding?

_____

9. How many shells did you see?

_____

10. What is Norah putting on?

_____

I DON'T WANNA!

To learn more about complaining, check out devotion 30 in The Wonder of Creation.

I don't wanna be the tree! This crown is too tight! Scientists say we complain about once every 60 seconds. And when we complain, our brain's neurons create shortcuts to make complaining even easier! Yikes! Thankfully, our brains create shortcuts for praising too. So the more we praise God, the easier it gets!

Look at these two pictures of Adelynn and Norah in the play. There are six differences. Can you spot them all?

SOUNDS LiKE . . .

To learn more about ears, check out devotion 17 in Indescribable.

Ears work by capturing sound waves in the *pinna* (PIN-uh), or outer ear. Those waves funnel down into the middle ear, where they turn into vibrations. Then they travel to the eardrum, the *cochlea* (KOH-klee-uh) of the inner ear, and finally the brain, which tells you what you're hearing.

In movies, people called *Foley artists* use everyday objects to make sounds for what's happening on-screen (called *sound effects*). For example, Foley artists might snap two leather gloves together to make a sound like a bat's wings flapping. Or they might break a piece of uncooked lasagna for a snapping twig. Be your own Foley artist and try using everyday objects to recreate the sounds below.

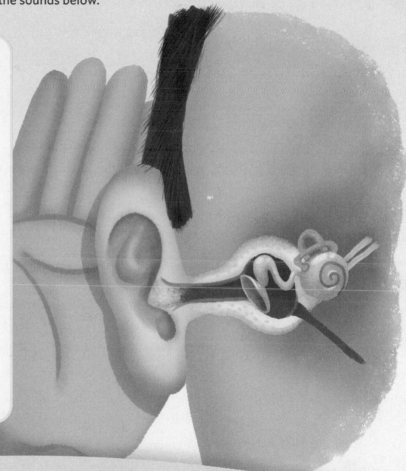

1. A creaking door
2. A dinosaur running
3. A horse trotting
4. A bird rustling its feathers
5. Dripping water
6. Rain
7. Waves
8. Walking through snow
9. Walking on leaves
10. Wind blowing through the trees
11. Thunder
12. A lion's roar

WHO ARE YOU LiSTENING TO?

Look up these verses and fill in the blanks to learn more about listening to God and His Word.

1. Do what God's teaching says; do not just _____ and do nothing. —James 1:22 ICB

2. So _____ comes from hearing the Good News. And people hear the Good

   News when someone tells them about _____. —Romans 10:17 ICB

3. Always be willing to listen and _____ to speak. Do not become _____ easily. —James 1:19 ICB

IT'S HOT AROUND HERE!

To learn more about the equator, check out devotion 96 in How Great Is Our God.

Did you know that there's an imaginary line around the Earth? Unscramble the words and place them in the paragraph below to learn all about that line. For an extra challenge, cover up the word bank.

BELT	EARTH	HOTTER	MOISTURE	RAYS
DIFFERENT	EQUATOR	MILES	RAIN	WEATHER

There's an imaginary line around the **rEaht** _____ called the **toruqea** _____. It circles
1   2

the center of the Earth—like a **ltbe** _____—between the North and South Poles. That belt is
3

about 24,900 **ilesm** _____ around!
4

Because the Earth is round and a little tilted in space, the Sun's **ysra** _____ fall straight down on
5

the equator. That makes the **thweera** _____ stay warm all year long—between 68 and 86 degrees
6

Fahrenheit in most places. The equator also gets about 80 inches of **iarn** _____ a year. All that
7

stuermio _____ in the air makes it feel much **ettrho** _____!
8   9

The equator is **erdifentf** _____ from the rest of the Earth
10

because it spends more time in the Sun. And when you spend more

time with Jesus the *Son*, you'll be different from the rest of the world

too. You'll be more like Him (2 Corinthians 3:18)!

JOKES!

What do you call a dog at the equator?	*A hot dog*
What do you call a snowman at the equator?	*A puddle*
Which is faster: heat or cold?	*Heat, because you can catch a cold!*

MISSION ACCOMPLISHED!

To learn more about the Apollo 11 mission to the Moon, check out devotion 87 in How Great Is Our God.

In 1961, President John F. Kennedy declared the United States was on a mission to put a man on the Moon. There were plenty of problems and challenges. But on July 20, 1969, astronauts Neil Armstrong and Buzz Aldrin walked on the Moon. Mission accomplished!

God has a mission for you too. He wants you to love Him and others (Matthew 22:37–40). There will be plenty of problems and challenges. Trust Him to help you, and one day you'll hear Him say, "Mission accomplished!" (Matthew 25:21).

Try these mini missions. How many can you complete?

1. Turn off all your "screens" for a day and spend time with God instead.

2. Ask God to show you who needs a smile and a kind word today.

3. With a grown-up's help, bake cookies for the fire department. Deliver them with a card that says, "I'm praying for you!"

4. Create a "care kit" with things like water, socks, and soap for someone in need. Ask your parents to help you find someone to give it to.

5. Call your grandparents just to chat.

6. Hug your mom and dad just because you love them.

7. Thank God for at least five things every night this week before you go to bed.

8. Before you get up in the morning—before you even get out of bed—tell God how wonderful He is.

9. If a friend is having a tough day, pray with them.

10. When others are talking, be a good listener.

11. Look for things other people are good at doing and praise them for it.

12. If someone is being left out, invite them to join you.

WHIRL AND SWIRL

To learn more about whirlpools, check out devotion 77 in How Great Is Our God.

Whirlpools are swirling funnels of water—like the tiny one Adelynn is watching. Some are bigger and swirl around so fast that they can pull objects down inside them. The most powerful kind is called a *maelstrom* (MAIL-struhm), and it can even sink small boats!

Use a pencil to navigate your way through the swirling waters to the bottom of the whirlpool.

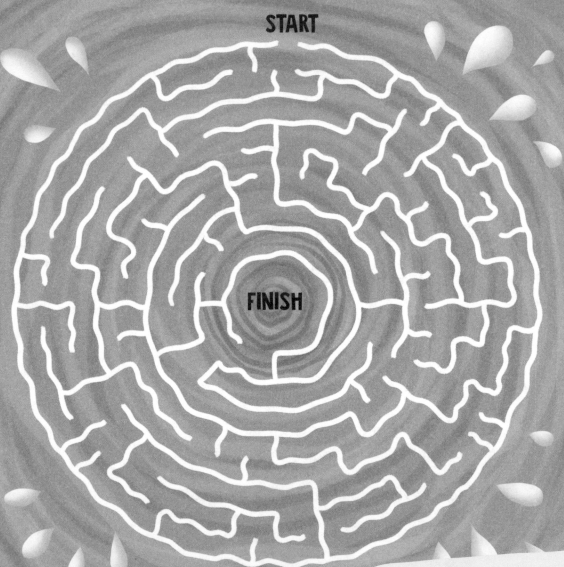

START

FINISH

Sometimes life feels like a whirlpool, with troubles and problems swirling all around. Call out to Jesus. He can calm the wind, waves, and whirlpools of trouble (Mark 4:35–41)!

STRAIGHT UP TO SPACE

To learn more about the Karman Line, check out devotion 52 in How Great Is Our God.

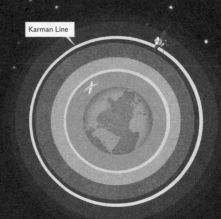
Karman Line

The Karman Line is an invisible line that marks the end of Earth's atmosphere and the beginning of space. It's only about 50 miles above the Earth's surface. That means, if you could drive a car straight up, you'd be in space in less than an hour!

Match a picture and a word to make a space term. Can you find all nine?

ASTRO

WAY

FULL

+Y

OFF

SPACE

BLACK

SHOOTING

YEAR

SPACE

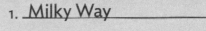

1. <u>Milky Way</u>

2. _____

3. _____

4. _____

5. _____

6. _____

7. _____

8. _____

9. _____

Sometimes you might feel like God is as far away as space, especially when you're hurting or upset. But He's not. God is with you every second (Matthew 28:20)!

GET IT OUT

To learn more about what stress does, check out devotion 6 in The Wonder of Creation.

It's the day of the big game. Your heart is pounding, your hands are sweaty, and you feel like you might be sick. But you're not sick. You're stressed! Stress is what happens to your body when you feel worried, nervous, afraid, or angry.

To calm down, you need to get that stress out of your body. Talk it out with God. Breathe it out with slow, deep breaths. Or write it out in a journal. Getting everything down on paper can help you figure out what you need to do.

Use these prompts to write about whatever is stressing you.

Today, I keep thinking about . . .

_____

_____

I feel . . .

_____

_____

One thing I can do to make this situation better is . . .

_____

_____

Someone I can talk to about this is . . .

_____

_____

I am grateful for . . .

_____

_____

God promises to never leave me (Joshua 1:9) and always help me (Psalm 46:1). That makes me feel . . .

_____

_____

Write out a prayer asking God to calm you and help you through this.

_____

_____

_____

QUICK CHALLENGE

When stress makes it hard to breathe, try slowing down and taking a look around. Then name five things you can see, four things you can touch, three things you can hear, two things you can smell, and one thing you can taste. Doing this will help you relax!

WHAT A FACE!

To learn more about the sawfish, check out devotion 91 in The Wonder of Creation.

That chainsaw-looking thing on the sawfish's face is called a *rostrum* (RAH-strum). God filled it with thousands of sensors to help the sawfish track down its prey. Then, with a sword-like *swish-swish*, it's lunchtime for the sawfish!

Use your crayons to color this picture of a sawfish in the sea.

STUCK TOGETHER

To learn more about spiderwebs, check out devotion 61 in How Great Is Our God.

Each strand of a spiderweb is made of thousands of smaller strands, called *nanostrands*. All those nanostrands together make spiderwebs super-strong—as much as five times stronger than steel!

Help the spider through the maze of its web to reach the other side.

When God's people all stick together, it's called *unity*. Without unity, we can get stuck in a maze of quarrels. But when we love and care for each other, it helps us be super-strong (Ephesians 4:1–3).

BRIGHT LiGHTS

To learn more about things that glow in the dark, check out devotion 45 in How Great Is Our God.

Chemiluminescence (keh-muh-loo-muh-NES-uhnts) is a reaction between chemicals, and it's the process that makes glow sticks glow. Thin glass tubes inside the glow stick keep the chemicals separate until you bend it. Then the tubes are broken, and the chemicals mix, creating the glow.

But do glow sticks always glow with the same brightness? Is it possible for water or temperature to affect how brightly they glow? Or how long they glow? Try this experiment and find out!

Supplies

- 3 clear glasses
- water
- ice
- 4 glow sticks
- watch or clock

> When our tempers are hot, it's tougher to "glow" with the light and love of Jesus. But that's just what He wants us to do (Ephesians 4:26; Ephesians 5:8). Ask Him, and He'll help you!

Steps

1. Fill one glass with ice and water. Fill another with lukewarm water. And with a grown-up's help, fill the third glass with hot water from the faucet (not boiling).

2. Snap and shake the glow sticks.

3. Drop one glow stick into each glass. Lay the fourth on the table in front of the glasses.

4. Observe what happens. Does one glow brighter or longer? Record the results in the chart.

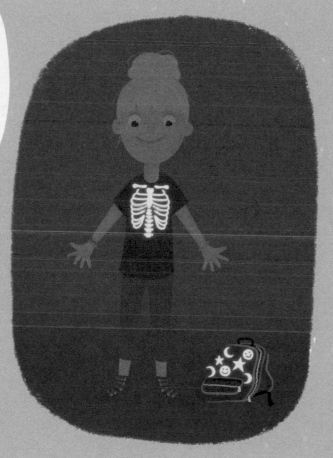

	Which glows brightest?	How long does it glow?
Hot water		
Lukewarm water		
Ice water		
No water		

TWISTERS!

To learn more about tornadoes, check out devotion 61 in Indescribable.

Tornadoes—or twisters—are terrifying! They are funnels of fast-spinning air that stretch from the clouds down to the ground. Wind speeds of tornadoes can vary from 40 to more than 300 miles an hour!

Make Your Own Tornado in a Bottle

Supplies
- clear plastic water bottle
- water
- liquid dish soap
- glitter

Steps
1. Fill the water bottle about 3/4 full of water.

2. Add a few drops of dish soap.

3. Add a pinch or two of glitter.

4. Put the cap on tightly and make sure it doesn't leak.

5. Turn the bottle upside down and hold it by the "neck." Spin the bottle in a circle for a few seconds. Stop and watch the water. Do you see the mini tornado forming in the glitter?

God is even stronger than the most powerful wind. After all, He created it (Amos 4:13)!

LiFE iN THE DESERT?

To learn more about the desert, check out devotion 26 in How Great Is Our God.

The Sahara Desert is one of Earth's largest deserts. Temperatures can range from near freezing at night to over 117 degrees Fahrenheit in the daytime. Yet God filled the Sahara with over 500 different species of plants and animals!

This picture of desert life has some missing pieces. Complete the picture by writing the letter of the correct piece in each space.

A   B   C   D   E   F

NO ROBOT LIKE YOU

To learn more about robots, check out devotion 41 in The Wonder of Creation.

Today's robots are doing incredible things! Like the Ameca robot. It can raise its eyebrows, smile, and even scratch its nose. But it can't walk. No matter how amazing robots get, they'll never do all the things God created you to do!

Follow these steps to learn how to draw a robot.

What has God created you to do? Look up Micah 6:8 to find out just part of God's purpose for you.

NOW DRAW A LARGE ROBOT ON THIS PAGE.

ZOOMING ON THE INFORMATION SUPERHIGHWAY

To learn more about the internet, check out devotion 8 in The Wonder of Creation.

The internet is a network of computers all linked together with a kind of digital "road,"
which is why it's sometimes called the "information superhighway." You can access the
internet almost anywhere in the world—even on top of Mount Everest!

Every word in this list is connected to the internet. Can you find them all?

```
R D Q E B F J D Y H T T V E I
Y E O D N C T Q A X L J I T N
A T T W D I B V E O J N D I F
W W T U N Y G T K C A H E S O
H O Q O P L F N R Z U M O B R
G R N O P M O S E H U C S E M
I L F R U S O A G H I E S W A
H D E L W D E C D A C I M I T
R W D I G I T A L C M R N C I
E I O A Z W K M V E R T A V O
P D D M J M E M N Q E H J E N
U E P E F D Y I N R N Z Z H S
S W J X I O L X N Z Q D U D H
D E A A Q N Y E Z S E F R X C
V B K R O A T U U W R F E Y C
```

COMPUTER	**HACK**	**SEARCH ENGINE**	**TEXT**
DIGITAL	**INFORMATION**	**SOCIAL MEDIA**	**VIDEOS**
DOWNLOAD	**INTERNET**	**SUPERHIGHWAY**	**WEBSITE**
EMAIL	**ONLINE**	**SURF**	**WORLD WIDE WEB**

Like any road trip, it's good to have a guide when you zoom along
on the internet—or you might end up somewhere you really
don't want to be! Philippians 4:8 is a great guide. Check it out!

A LiGHT TO "SEA" BY

To learn more about glowing seas, check out devotion 52 in The Wonder of Creation.

For centuries, scientists refused to believe sailors' stories of mysterious, glowing seas. But in 2005, satellite pictures proved their tales were true! What caused the glow? Billions and billions of *bioluminescent* (bye-oh-loo-muh-NES-uhnt) bacteria, which can create their own light!

Connect the dots to see what's floating in these glowing seas!

Start here

Scientists didn't believe those sailors' stories until they saw the glow with their own eyes. A lot of people feel that way about God and His love. But you can help people "see" God's love by the way you love others (John 13:35).

MISSION TO JUPITER

To learn more about Jupiter, check out devotion 90 in The Wonder of Creation.

Jupiter is a gigantic swirling mass of gases, making it difficult to explore. In 2011, NASA launched the Juno spacecraft to take a closer look. It arrived in 2016 and has been transmitting pictures from its JunoCam ever since.

Imagine JunoCam transmitted a picture so unbelievable that NASA sent a crew of astronauts to investigate—and you're one of them! Finish the story below and describe what you find.

ASTRONAUT'S LOGBOOK

My fellow astronauts and I are aboard the Juno 2 on an emergency mission from NASA. It's only day two of our orbit around Jupiter, and our instruments are going crazy! I thought they must have malfunctioned, but then I looked out the window. That's when I knew the pictures were real! Because rising out of the swirling gases of the massive planet was . . .

God already knows everything about Jupiter—and everything about everything (Psalm 147:5)! So when we ask Him for help, we can trust His answer will be just what we need.

A STRANGE PLACE TO LIVE

To learn more about clownfish, check out devotion 98 in How Great Is Our God.

The clownfish makes its home right in the middle of the poisonous stinging tentacles of the *sea anemone* (uh-NEM-uh-nee). But don't worry! God gave the clownfish a special layer of mucus on its skin to protect it from the anemone's stings.

Color in the spaces using the color code to see who's hiding in this underwater scene.

FLOWER POWER

To learn more about plants' defenses, check out devotion 32 in How Great Is Our God.

If you're in danger, you can run away. But for plants, running isn't an option. That's why God gave plants different ways to defend themselves and get the resources they need to survive. Check out these plants and their defenses.

Solve the sudoku puzzle by filling in each square with a plant. Include a rose, cactus, nettle, sunflower, painted daisy, and daffodil in each row, each column, and each six-square box.

Rose: Its stems have sharp thorns that poke any animals looking for a snack.

Cactus: This plant is covered in sharp, prickly spines—sometimes up to six inches long!

Nettle: Its tiny, needle-like hairs inject stinging chemicals into the skin of anything that touches it.

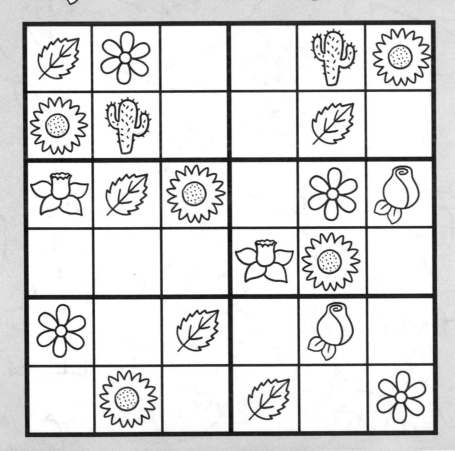

Sunflower: It uses up so much water and nutrients that other plants struggle to grow near it.

Painted daisy: It protects itself—and nearby plants—by making *pyrethrins* (pie-REE-thruns), natural chemicals that repel bugs and other animals.

Daffodil: Every part of this plant is poisonous, so animals quickly learn to leave it alone.

PRAYING, NOT PREYING

To learn more about the praying mantis, check out devotion 7 in How Great Is Our God.

Norah has discovered that this praying mantis isn't really praying; it's waiting for *prey*. This *ambush predator* waits quietly for a tasty bug, frog, or even bird to come by. Then it strikes with lightning-fast, ninja-like moves. *Dinnertime*!

With the Lord's Prayer, Jesus teaches us how to actually pray—not just look like we're praying. But this prayer has gotten all mixed up! Can you write it in the right order? (Hint: Look up Matthew 6:9–13 NLT for a little help.)

May your will be done on earth,
Our Father in heaven,
as it is in heaven.
May your Kingdom come soon.
but rescue us from the evil one.
and forgive us our sins,
may your name be kept holy.
as we have forgiven those who sin against us.
Give us today the food we need,
And don't let us yield to temptation,
—Matthew 6:9–13 NLT

1. _____

2. _____

3. _____

4. _____

5. _____

6. _____

7. _____

8. _____

9. _____

10. _____

—Matthew 6:9–13 NLT

PRAYING PATTERNS

God wants us to pray continually (1 Thessalonians 5:17). Try these tips to help you remember to pray:

1. Pray at the same time every day, like when you wake up or go to bed.
2. Create a special place to pray—in your room, in a closet, on the porch, or even by a special tree.
3. Keep a prayer journal. Write down what you pray about and keep a record of how God answers your prayers. Be sure to thank Him!
4. Pray every time you hear or see a certain thing, like praying for the sick every time you hear an ambulance siren.

ALWAYS MOVING

There's more going on in the air than what you think! Air is actually full of molecules that are constantly moving around. Those moving molecules push and pull on objects like kites, birds, and airplanes to make them move through the air.

Color this picture of a "flying" scene!

Air is always moving, even if you can't see it. Kind of like God! You may not see Him, but He's always moving and working in your life—for good (John 5:17)!

WHICH FRUIT IS FASTEST?

To learn more about fruit, check out devotion 27 in How Great Is Our God.

God created some fruits to grow on trees, like apples, oranges, and peaches. Others grow on bushes or small plants, like raspberries and strawberries. And still others grow on vines, like watermelons and grapes.

Different fruit seeds grow at different rates. Try this experiment to see how fast different fruits grow.

Supplies

- scissors
- paper towels
- water
- 5 seeds of 3 different kinds of fruit, such as watermelon, cantaloupe, apple, zucchini, orange, or tomato
- sandwich-size plastic bags
- permanent marker
- tape
- a sunny window

Steps

1. Cut a paper towel into three long pieces and wet each piece with water.

2. Put 5 seeds (of the same kind!) on the end of a paper towel piece and fold the other end over the seeds. Put the paper towel inside a plastic bag and seal it up. Use the marker to write what kind of seed is in the bag.

3. Repeat step 2 with the other two kinds of seeds.

4. Tape the bags to a sunny window.

5. Check the seeds each day for the next 3 weeks. If the paper towels dry out, open the bags and add enough water to make the paper towel damp.

6. Which seed sprouts first? Which one grows a leaf first? Record your observations below.

	Date of day 1:	Date seed sprouts:	Date first leaf appears:	How does it look on day 10?	How does it look on day 14?	How does it look on day 21?
Seed 1 _____						
Seed 2 _____						
Seed 3 _____						

IN THE KNOW ABOUT H₂O

To learn more about water, check out devotion 98 in Indescribable.

Water—or as scientists call it, H_2O—is a must-have for life. Maybe that's why God covered almost 70 percent of the Earth with water!

Answer these questions to fill in the crossword puzzle with more facts about water.

ACROSS
4. Almost all the Earth's water is stored in the Earth's _____.
5. Liquid H_2O is called _____.
8. Most of the Earth's *freshwater* is locked up in ice and giant frozen _____.

Our bodies need water—H_2O—to survive. But our souls need the living water of the Holy Spirit. How do we get that water? Believe and follow Jesus (John 7:37–39)!

DOWN
1. Water _____ at 212 degrees Fahrenheit.
2. Ice doesn't sink; it _____ on water.
3. Frozen water is called _____.
4. Water is made up of two atoms of hydrogen and one atom of _____.
6. Water can be a liquid, solid, or _____.
7. A person can survive almost a month without food but less than a _____ without water.

SPOT THE DiFFERENCE

Take a close look at these "watery" pictures. Circle the one that isn't quite like the others.

HEART WORK

To learn more about the heart, check out devotion 93 in Indescribable.

Your heart beats about 100,000 times a day to pump blood and all its life-giving nutrients throughout your body. And it never takes a break—not even when you're asleep!

But having a "heart for God" has nothing to do with your heartbeats. It means loving God and the people He created (Matthew 22:36–39). Review the list of ways you can have a heart for God and His people. Check off each one you're able to complete!

❑ 1. Before school starts, pray for all the students and teachers.

❑ 2. Talk to a parent about setting up a food pantry at school or in your neighborhood. Ask friends or neighbors to help stock it with things like macaroni and cheese, granola bars, and peanut butter.

❑ 3. Collect coats and blankets for a homeless shelter.

❑ 4. Collect old towels for an animal shelter.

❑ 5. Be a friend to someone who is different from you. (It won't take long to see you're not that different after all!)

❑ 6. Decorate your school folders with Bible verses so you can share God's Word without saying a word.

❑ 7. With your parents' permission, invite friends to help box up food at a food bank.

❑ 8. If someone comes to you with a problem, listen and then offer to pray with them.

❑ 9. Be a good example to those around you by being honest, kind, and helpful.

❑ 10. Add you own idea: _____

_____

A PROMISE IN THE SKY

To learn more about rainbows, check out devotion 75 in Indescribable.

Rainbows form when light from the Sun bends and bounces through water droplets in the air. To remember the colors of a rainbow, think of ROY G. BIV, which stands for Red, Orange, Yellow, Green, Blue, Indigo, and Violet.

There's a pattern in this rainbow of colors that looks like this: ➡ How fast can you find the pattern?

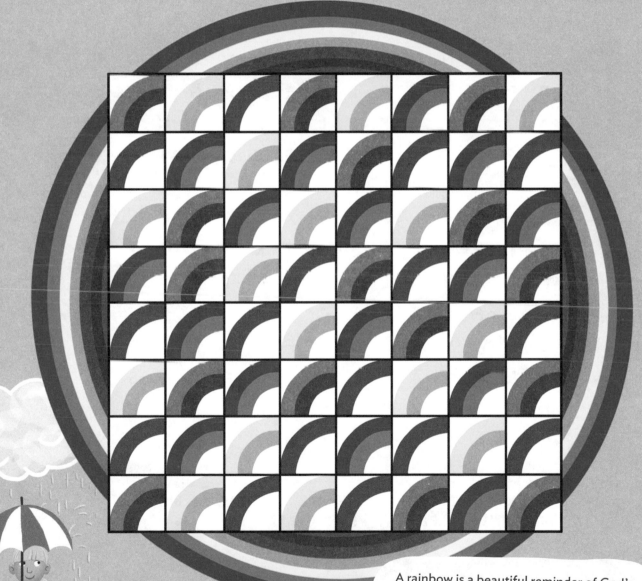

A rainbow is a beautiful reminder of God's promise to never again flood the entire Earth. Even more beautiful is the fact that God still keeps this promise—and every promise He's ever made (Proverbs 30:5)!

A GRAVEYARD OF SHIPS

To learn more about the Skeleton Coast, check out devotion 88 in The Wonder of Creation.

The coast of Namibia, a country in southern Africa, is littered with the "bones" of so many shipwrecks that it's called the Skeleton Coast. But this graveyard for ships also has one of the richest varieties of wildlife anywhere on the planet, from lions and elephants to kudus and seals.

Search through the letters below. Can you find all these words connected to the Skeleton Coast?

```
C S L A F A S L H Y O D Q A P
G H V L K C B Y D O U R Q S D
I I E U Q I Y X V N V I L N Y
R P D E P R L A E S H G L K K
A U I L T F E L E P H A N T S
F G Z O S A V O G X W B J C X
F U R N R L H H Q L X Z B G I
E A O A A C S V Z A U N C K T
C I R M V X S T H K G S Q S P
L L E B W E G W D C J D A Y E
I P F P E P Y O W A N O R Z V
L B W B Z Z A F J C L V Q N
K R Y E A K C E R W P I H S Z
I N D E Z G H M Y D N P T C H
C J A G E Q N A M I B I A T X
```

AFRICA	DUNE	GIRAFFE	KUDU	SHIP
CHEETAH	ELEPHANT	GRAVEYARD	LION	SHIPWRECK
COAST	FOG	JACKAL	SEAL	ZEBRA

When your day is feeling "wrecked," pray this prayer from Scripture: "Lord, tell me your ways. Show me how to live. . . . I trust you all day long" (Psalm 25:4–5).

GO AHEAD AND LAUGH

To learn more about laughter, check out devotion 18 in How Great Is Our God.

You don't have to learn to laugh. In fact, babies start laughing at just three months old! The science of laughing is called *gelotology* (jell-oh-TOL-oh-gee), and those who study it say that laughter not only makes people happier, but it also gets rid of your stress and helps you think better.

Look up these joyful Bible verses using the International Children's Bible and fill in the missing words.

God will yet fill your mouth with _____. And he will fill your lips with shouts of _____. —Job 8:21

A happy _____ is like good _____. —Proverbs 17:22

Then we were filled with _____, and we sang _____ songs. Then the other nations said, "The Lord has done _____ things for them." —Psalm 126:2

There is a time to _____ and a time to _____. —Ecclesiastes 3:4

"I have told you these things so that you can have the same _____ I have. I want your _____ to be the fullest _____." —John 15:11

"So you will go out with joy. You will be led out in peace. The _____ and hills will burst into song before you. All the _____ in the fields will clap their hands." —Isaiah 55:12

TO LAUGH OR NOT TO LAUGH

Scientists don't fully understand what makes some jokes funny and others not. Often it's because we're surprised by the ending. Other times there is a funny twist to the words, like the joke about a cheetah—or cheater—below. Check out these jokes, then try making up a joke or two of your own!

What animal did Noah not trust? — *The cheetah.*

On the ark, Noah may have gotten milk from the cows. What did he get from the ducks? — *Quackers!*

How do you cut the sea in half? — *With a sea-saw!*

What kind of tree will fit in your hand? — *A palm tree.*

How did the astronaut serve dinner? — *On flying saucers.*

FOLLOW THAT NOSE!

To learn more about bloodhounds, check out devotion 47 in How Great Is Our God.

Bloodhounds are often called the "nose with a dog attached." Their amazing noses have between 250 and 300 million scent receptors—humans have only about 400. A bloodhound can follow a scent trail that's 300 hours old. That's almost 13 days!

Take a close look at these pictures. Circle the one that isn't like the rest.

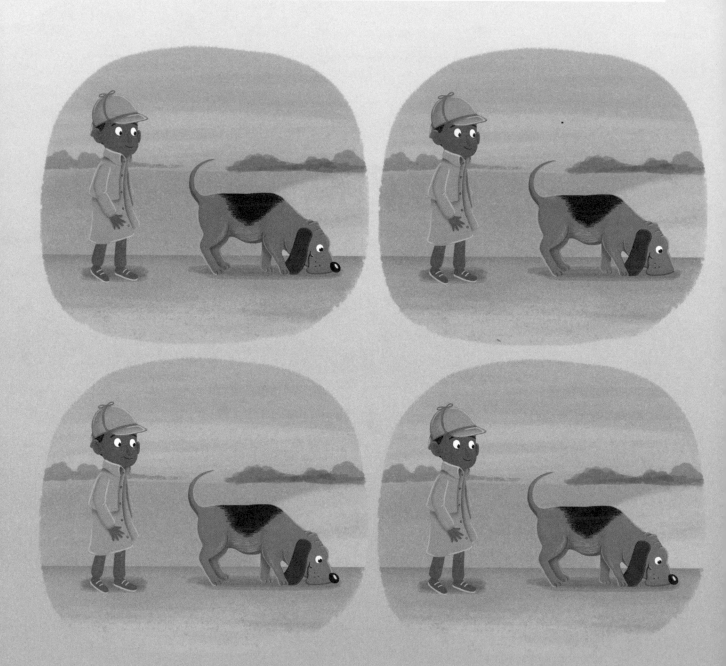

THE NOSE KNOWS

To learn more about bloodhounds, check out devotion 47 in How Great Is Our God.

Fill in these blanks to complete the crossword puzzle and learn more about bloodhounds.

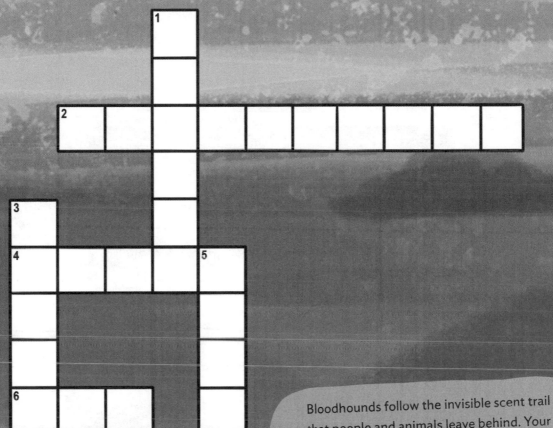

Bloodhounds follow the invisible scent trail that people and animals leave behind. Your words and actions also leave behind a trail. Do they "stink" with gossip and selfishness? Or do they have the sweet scent of love and kindness that leads others to God (John 13:35)?

ACROSS
2. When a bloodhound smells a person's clothing, it creates an "odor image"—like a _____ or picture—of that person.
4. A bloodhound can follow a scent trail for more than 130 _____!
6. The bloodhound's ability to track is so good that it's accepted in a court of _____.

DOWN
1. Bloodhounds are often used to track down missing _____.
3. A bloodhound's sense of _____ is about 1,000 times stronger than a human's.
5. A person's odor image includes things like sweat, breath, and _____ (the outer layer of our bodies).

UP, UP, AND AWAY!

How does a solid airplane, weighing thousands of pounds, fly through air that feels like it weighs nothing at all? It depends on four invisible forces working together: weight, lift, thrust, and drag.

Weight: This includes the weight of the plane, passengers, luggage, and fuel.

Lift: Air is filled with little molecules. As an airplane's wing pushes those molecules down, the air lifts up the plane.

Thrust: This is caused by the propellers or jet engine that push the plane forward.

Drag: Air pushing against the plane as it moves forward is drag. An airplane is smooth and rounded, so there isn't much drag—until it's ready to land. Then flaps pop up on the wings to increase drag and slow the plane down.

Follow these steps to learn how to draw an airplane.

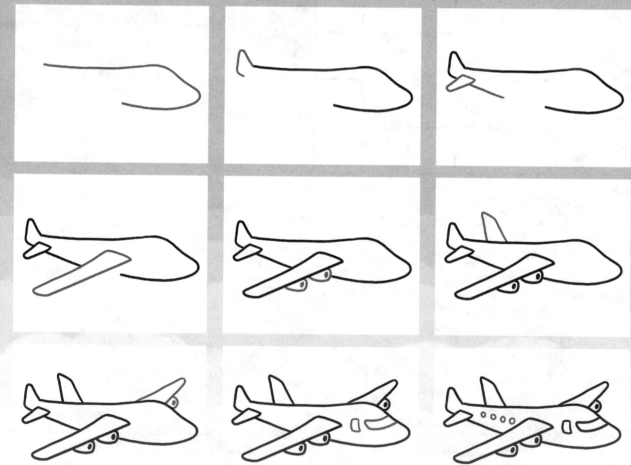

DRAW AN AIRPLANE HERE, THEN COLOR IN THIS FLYING SCENE.

Three of the most powerful forces in our world are invisible. Look up 1 Corinthians 13:13 to discover what they are.

CORAL CREATIONS

To learn more about coral, check out devotion 58 in How Great Is Our God.

God created enormous elephants and whopping-big whales. But He also created teeny- tiny animals. Like coral. That's right, coral is an animal! Or rather, coral is made up of thousands of tiny animals called *polyps* (POL-ups) all living together.

In Joshua's underwater picture below, some of the pieces are missing. Complete the picture by writing the number of the correct piece in each space.

DiD YOU HEAR THAT?

To learn more about bats and echolocation, check out devotion 65 in How Great Is Our God.

Echolocation (EH-koh-loh-KAY-shun) is the process of using sound waves—or vibrations—to locate things. God created some animals (like bats, dolphins, and whales) to use echolocation to help them find prey, navigate, and avoid enemies.

Try this experiment to see how sound waves work.

Supplies

- metal spoon
- about 4 feet or more of yarn or string
- ruler
- a friend

Steps

1. Tie the spoon to the middle of the string.

2. Wrap one end of the string a few times around the index finger of your left hand—not too tight! Wrap the other end around the index finger of your right hand.

3. Raise your hands up so that your fingers are close to your ears and the spoon hangs down by your tummy.

4. Ask a friend to tap the spoon with the ruler.

What do you hear? Does the sound change if you move your fingers closer to or farther away from your ears? Record your observations below.

_____

_____

_____

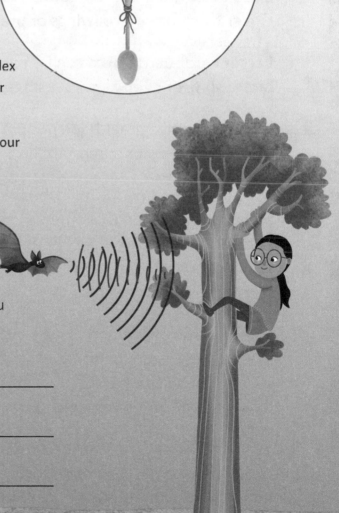

CLEAN UP THE JUNK

To learn more about space junk, check out devotion 86 in The Wonder of Creation.

Millions of pieces of junk are zooming around space—from old satellites to an astronaut's dropped glove. Scientists hope to clean up space with robots like OSCaR, or Obsolete Spacecraft Capture and Removal. Fleets of these shoebox-sized robots would shoot out nets to capture all that junk.

Here on Earth, we can clean up the space around us by figuring out new ways to use our old junk. It's called *upcycling*. It's great for the environment and your imagination!

1. Turn soup or vegetable cans into flowerpots. Just clean and fill with dirt. Add flower seeds, a little water, and sunshine.

2. Shoeboxes are great for storing craft supplies and small toys. Cover the box with drawings or pretty paper.

3. Larger cardboard boxes can be combined to make a fort, a pirate ship, or even a puppet stage.

4. Old socks make great hand puppets. Glue on button eyes, a pom-pom nose, or some yarn hair—whatever you imagine!

5. Make new crayons from old, broken ones. Remove the paper and put the broken crayons in the bottom of a muffin tin. With a grown-up's help, bake at 275 degrees Fahrenheit for 10–12 minutes. Remove after they completely cool. Then start coloring!

6. Use a plastic milk jug to make a catch-and-throw game. With a grown-up's help, cut off the bottom inch of the jug, leaving you with a handle and "cup." Take turns with a friend tossing a ball and trying to catch it in the "cup."

7. Turn a toilet paper roll into a bird feeder. Thread a piece of yarn or heavy string through the middle of an empty toilet paper roll, then tie a knot. Cover the tube with peanut butter, roll it in birdseed, then hang it by the string outside.

Taking care of the Earth is one of the jobs God gave us right from the start (Genesis 1:26). How can you take care of His creation today?

AROUND AND AROUND AND AROUND!

To learn more about how the Earth moves, check out devotion 16 in How Great Is Our God.

You might think you're standing still, but actually you're spinning around—and around and around! That's because the Earth is spinning in space at a speed of about 1,000 miles per hour. Feeling dizzy yet?

Take a close look at this picture of Earth and all the Indescribable kids. Can you find all the hidden images?

God has placed you in just the right spot on this spinning planet to tell everyone around you about His love!

INDEX

ACTIVITY TYPE

INDESCRIBABLE KIDS DEVOTIONALS

SUBJECT

ANSWERS

Page 5: Mountain Maze

Page 6: The Eyes Have It

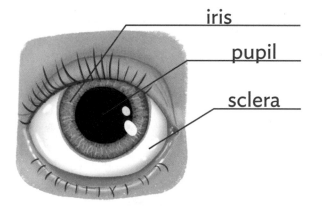

iris
pupil
sclera

lens
retina
optic nerve
vitreous humor
ciliary muscles

Page 7: Putting the Pieces Together

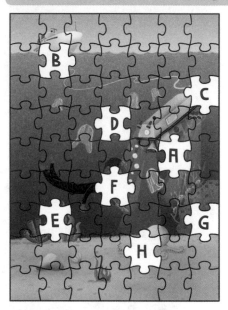

Pages 8–9: Just the Facts

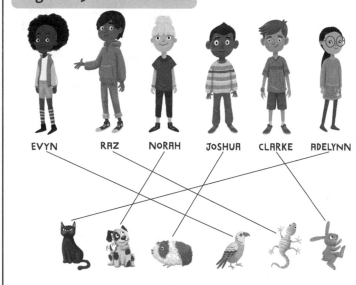

EVYN   RAZ   NORAH   JOSHUA   CLARKE   ADELYNN

	cat	dog	guinea pig	parakeet	gecko	rabbit
Evyn	X	X	X	O	X	X
Raz	X	X	X	X	O	X
Norah	X	O	X	X	X	X
Joshua	X	X	O	X	X	X
Clarke	X	X	X	X	X	O
Adelynn	O	X	X	X	X	X

Page 10: The Great Space Search

```
M H V N I R D L A Z Z U B Y S
O Y T I V A R G X S B S A R S
O C Q F G X V A X Z T S E N S
N H I O U K E S D S A T I O P
L T J M O Y T A I N A L B A A
A R Z S M E P T S R L J C E C
N A N Q K H N P C O K W W H E
D E B C C E A R C B O P F S C
I B O N I C A L N E G E O K R
N R U C E N E J C W E O X O A
G A S R U A T N I R P T O O F
L B A L H S P A C E S U I T T
A C M C N H D W Z M O O N Q P
E M I S S I O N C O N T R O L
N M G N O R T S M R A L I E N
```

Page 11: Not Quite the Same

Page 19: It's a River of Life!

Page 22: Home Sweet Home

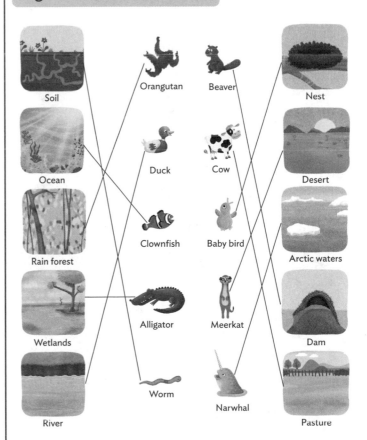

Page 23: Hold On!

Page 25: Crossing into Space

Across:
4. Moon
6. Milky Way
8. cracker
9. stars

Down:
1. light-year
2. Goldilocks
3. Sun
5. oxygen
7. gravity

Page 26: Bones, Bones, Bones

```
L M H U E W H T E L
U R A D I U S G A I
B L X C M U N T F W
S W N E I A C Z C K
V B R A L L U K S F
N U I A C G L Q S E
S K H R R K G F I M
Z P S A L T W D N U
H V W X A G O X X R
K F G X M I Z F M A
```

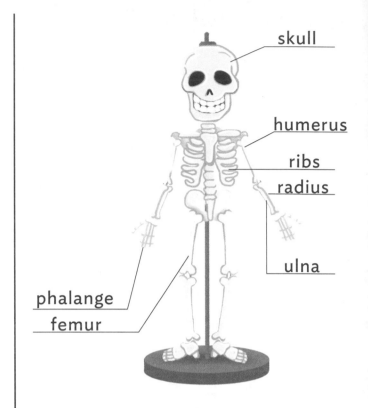

skull
humerus
ribs
radius
ulna
phalange
femur

Page 27: Squiggly, Wiggly

Page 28: Sheep Gotta Have a Shepherd

Page 29: Get the Picture?

$2 \times 2 = $ **4** $2 + 3 = $ **5**   **6** $6 + 1 = $ **7**

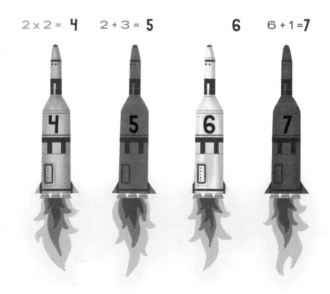

Ranger 7 took the pictures!

Page 30: A Fruity Puzzle

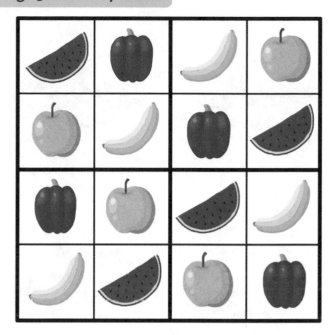

Page 31: Definitely Not a Banana

LOVE
JOY
PEACE
PATIENCE
KINDNESS
GOODNESS
FAITHFULNESS
GENTLENESS
SELF-CONTROL

You can wait without getting upset.

This is being thoughtful and nice to others.

A happy feeling lives in your heart, even when things aren't going your way.

This is the opposite of badness.

Being in control of what you do and say, even when you're upset or angry.

It's not just a feeling; it's the things you do. God wants your actions to show this—to Him and to your neighbors too.

This means you're loyal, you're dependable, and you keep your promises, just like God keeps His.

Being soft and kind— not harsh—with your words and actions.

A calm feeling that comes from knowing God loves you and trusting Him to take care of you.

Page 32: Living the High Life

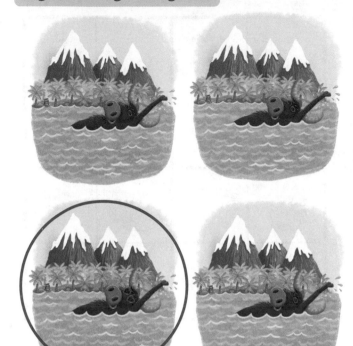

Pages 36–37: Busy Little Brains

1. 7
2. 1
3. 3
4. beehive
5. 2
6. blue
7. white
8. squirrels and a bird

Page 38: Colorful Creation

Page 41: When You're Happy and You Know It

Across:
4. mane
5. whiskers
7. tiger
8. leopard
10. roar

Down:
1. claws
2. meow
3. tail
6. kitten
9. purr

Page 42: Don't Break a Sweat

1. T
2. F
3. F
4. T
5. F
6. T
7. T

Page 43: Lions, Hippos, and Gorillas—Oh My!

```
D D Y T Q B W H E T I M B E R
J I R A I K B A L W B A E J G
W L A A L N H G E W O L V S W
W M V M P T V H P C U O P X V
A M C R O O I L H C O P P E R
D T M V N N E H A F D R M E Z
Q W O Z D X D L N Q T N B X Y
Y W T O S R B S T U Q B X Z N
U A L L I R O G D N U K Z L Y
B W D R D I B J V R J N Z S D
L Y F C N G M P Q I X D D C N
V C G S O S B J N K K S S U J
L Z K L I D B W J M T Y F X Z
A J D C L R W P I Q C A N F Y
P U K I K O H T C R F K F E A
```

Page 47: Just One Way

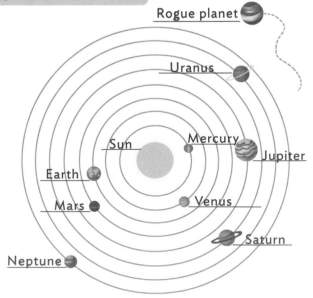

Page 52: Life in the Trees

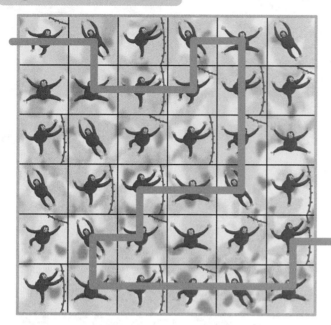

Page 53: Animals Everywhere!

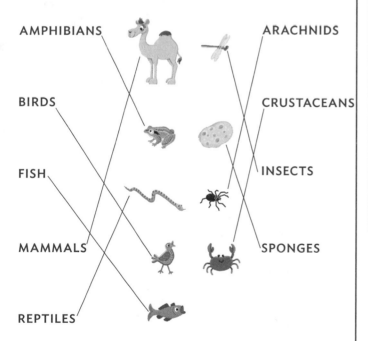

AMPHIBIANS

ARACHNIDS

BIRDS

CRUSTACEANS

FISH

INSECTS

MAMMALS

SPONGES

REPTILES

Page 54: That's No Star!

1. light
2. dust
3. asteroids
4. atmosphere
5. meteor
6. God
7. wish

Page 55: A Leafy Arrangement

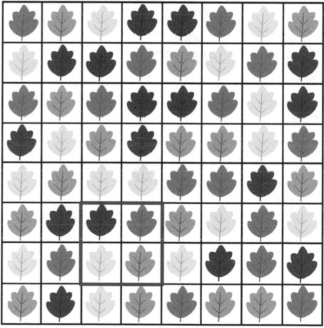

Page 56: By the Numbers

A. 9; B. 3; C. 4; D. 2

Many Sierra redwood trees are between **2**,000 and **3**,000 years old!

Some trees might even be over **4**,000 years old!

These amazing trees can grow to be **3**00 feet tall—that's about as tall as the Statue of Liberty!

And unless you have *really* long arms, you can't hug these trees. That's because their trunks can be more than **9 4** feet around!

Page 59: Moon on the Move

1. moon
2. Saturn
3. Titan
4. orbit
5. astronomers

E	I	D	L	K	Z	Y	S	H	S	W
P	N	W	L	X	D	V	P	M	R	X
W	M	Y	D	G	S	G	G	S	E	A
D	N	A	T	I	T	A	P	D	M	F
I	P	O	C	R	S	A	W	Y	O	E
F	Q	V	X	A	T	H	B	M	N	W
P	F	V	T	T	G	H	M	O	O	C
V	U	U	Q	E	I	N	U	O	R	S
D	R	B	O	U	O	B	K	N	T	Z
N	R	S	D	Q	B	P	R	K	S	U
T	O	Z	L	L	J	K	U	O	A	H

Page 61: Going Deep!

Page 64: Seeds on the Sea

Page 65: It's a Germ Invasion!

Page 66: Fuzzy, Furry, Feathered Friends

Page 70: The Great *What*?

1. solar system

2. orbit

3. Sun

4. Jupiter

5. twenty

6. Great

7. million

Page 70: Space Maze

Page 71: Small but Powerful!

1. Genesis 1

2. fight off diseases and digest food

3. chains of even smaller amino acids

4. 1 in 10 duodecillion (or a 1 with 40 zeros after it)

5. *answers may vary*

Page 73: The Goldilocks Zone

1. distance
2. water
3. rock
4. ozone, shields
5. atmosphere
6. Moon
7. heat, light
8. Jupiter
9. planets
10. Milky Way

Page 74: Important After All!

Across:
1. small
2. purpose
3. bacteria
5. digest

Down:
1. stomach
4. appendix

Page 75: Don't Give Up!

Page 76: More Than a Marble

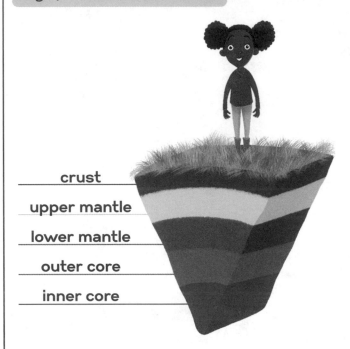

crust

upper mantle

lower mantle

outer core

inner core

Page 78: What's the Weather?

P	S	R	H	S	S	M	E	E	O
I	G	A	T	G	O	F	S	N	E
H	P	I	M	E	E	L	T	A	Y
N	W	N	A	F	E	I	C	C	S
D	R	A	Z	Z	I	L	B	I	C
F	R	X	W	R	L	V	S	R	E
I	J	E	W	O	N	I	T	R	K
Q	G	N	E	H	N	R	A	U	T
G	A	S	I	Q	N	S	I	H	P
W	E	J	R	A	P	I	H	U	S

Page 79: This Way!

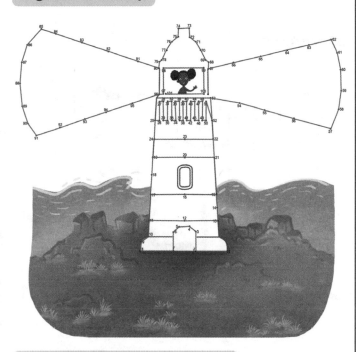

Page 83: A Not-So-Tasty Snack

1. monarch
2. orange
3. poisonous
4. milkweed
5. caterpillars
6. predator

Page 84: Hide and Seek!

Page 85: Could That Be True?

1. T
2. F
3. T
4. F
5. T

Page 86: All Mixed Up!

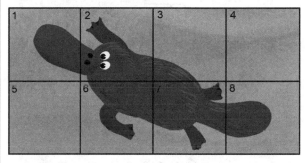

Pages 88–89: Do You Remember?

1. two of the following colors: purple, red, blue, or green
2. Peru
3. red
4. party hat
5. six
6. green
7. bear
8. soccer ball
9. skateboard or party hat
10. 132

Page 90: Like Glue!

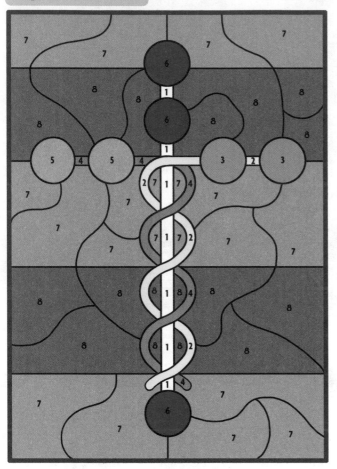

Page 92: Perfectly Planted

```
A Y V V F D E S E R T N Q S A
R E Z P Q X U Y R A L V T T B
H P M Q X N E E E X E F L N Z
N E Q J L A E M D J A L L E C
T G M I S D J H M Q V O B I K
Z X G R E T A W R R E V F R P
P H U B F F Q Z A O S A A T D
T J E P T A H I S A O D V U N
W I T R L Q N P Q M R T W N E
N Q I S Y F Z C G O J F S A X
K D C U O S E T Y H P I P E F
Y W B R J U G Y V B R A G X K
C Z E G V I A R O Y C B N M A
J S Z Q I H D I I L K W B H L
T E L M I W F D B A T Y A M R
```

Page 96: Happy Hopping

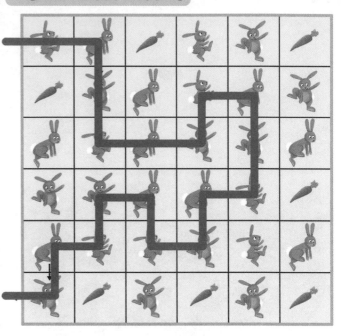

Page 97: Feeling a Little *Hangry*?

1. hungry
2. angry
3. hangry
4. attitude
5. body
6. sugars
7. energy
8. trouble
9. fight
10. flight
11. control

Page 100: Smile!

Across:
3. dentist
6. cavity
7. cheese
8. biting
10. floss

Down:
1. grinding
2. toothpaste
4. enamel
5. chew
8. bones
9. smile

Page 101: Happy Napping

1. NASA learned astronauts were happier, more creative, and more alert after a short nap
2. frigate
3. dolphins
4. about half of a day
5. otters hold on to seaweed—or other otters—to keep from drifting away

Pages 102–103: Clues in the Rock

1. *answers may vary*
2. jump across the stones
3. 12
4. climb down the ladder
5. *answers may vary*
6. water bottle
7. T. rex
8. soft paintbrush

Pages 104–105: It's *Elementary*!

2: helium

8: oxygen

11: sodium

20: calcium

26: iron

28: nickel

47: silver

79: gold

Page 106: Bless You!

Across:
3. organisms
4. pathogen
5. sneezes
9. microscope

Down:
1. germ
2. washing
6. elbow
7. water
8. sick
10. cough

Page 108: Just a *Little* Different

Page 109: *Cell*-ebration!

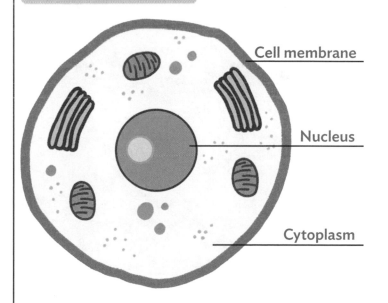

Page 110: Say, "Cheese!"

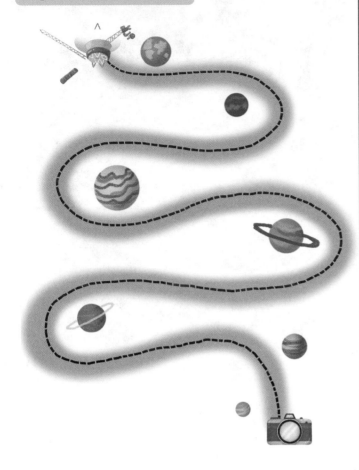

Page 115: Who's Been Here?

Page 111: Wherever You Go

1. fortress

2. turtles

3. shell

4. bones

5. scutes

6. spine

7. love

Page 116: Amazing Ants

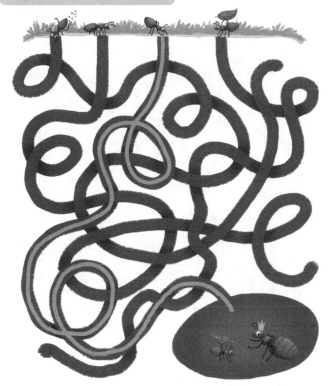

Page 118: Searching Cenotes

```
O D Z S W U A S W R K F
N S N I C A V E A H P D
A I E U L N Z C T C Z E
Y O U T O G T O E E C G
I R E J I R M L R N Z I
U F R I R M G R S T Q Q
P P C T A E G R B E N I
E X R M J E V A E R S K
T C U F O S S I L D R T
S I N K H O L E D A N T
V A T X D F C M D Y T U
S S E T I T C A L A T S
```

Page 119: On the Lookout!

Page 120: Now That's Hot!

1. T
2. F
3. F
4. T

Page 121: Volcano!

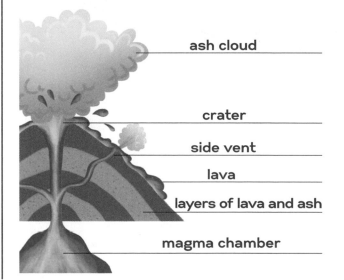

ash cloud

crater

side vent

lava

layers of lava and ash

magma chamber

Page 122: Reach for the Stars!

Across:
2. sailors
5. gas
6. space
7. twinkle
8. gravity
10. Sun

Down:
1. black
2. supernova
3. star
4. wish
8. God
9. years

Page 123: Way Under the Waves

D I S C O V E R

Page 124: A Colorful Warning

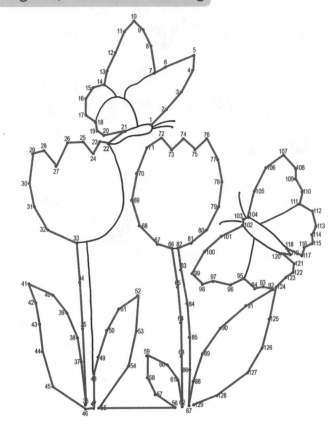

Pages 128–129: Count on It!

1. 9
2. blue
3. 4
4. 3
5. three of the following colors: green, blue, purple, or yellow
6. 4
7. 3
8. a flag
9. 5
10. sunscreen

Page 130: I Don't Wanna!

Page 131: Who Are You Listening To?

1. listen
2. faith, Christ
3. slow, angry

Page 132: It's Hot Around Here!

1. Earth
2. equator
3. belt
4. miles
5. rays
6. weather
7. rain
8. moisture
9. hotter
10. different

Page 134: Whirl and Swirl

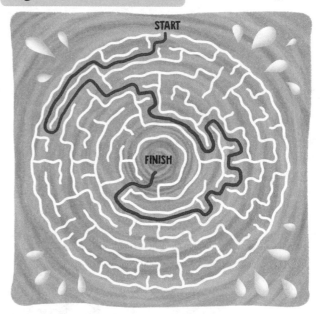

Page 135: Straight Up to Space

Order of answers may vary.

1. Milky Way
2. blast off
3. black hole
4. light-year
5. spaceship
6. full moon
7. space suit
8. astronaut
9. shooting star

Page 138: Stuck Together

Page 141: Life in the Desert?

Page 145: A Light to "Sea" By

Page 144: Zooming on the Information Superhighway

```
R D Q E B F J D Y H T T V E I
Y E O D N C T Q A X L J I T N
A T T W D I B V E O J N D I F
W W T U N Y G T K C A H E S O
H O Q O P L F N R Z U M O B R
G R N O P M O S E H U C S E M
I L F R U S O A G H I E S W A
H D E L W D E C D A C I M I T
R W D I G I T A L C M R N C I
E I O A Z W K M V E R T A V O
P D D M J M E M N Q E H J E N
U E P E F D Y I N R N Z Z H S
S W J X I O L X N Z Q D U D H
D E A A Q N Y E Z S E F R X C
V B K R O A T U U W R F E Y C
```

Page 147: A Strange Place to Live

Page 148: Flower Power

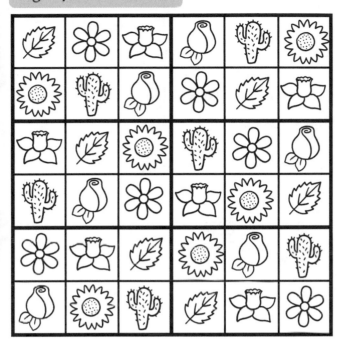

Page 149: Praying, Not Preying

1. Our Father in heaven,
2. may your name be kept holy.
3. May your Kingdom come soon.
4. May your will be done on earth,
5. as it is in heaven.
6. Give us today the food we need,
7. and forgive us our sins,
8. as we have forgiven those who sin against us.
9. And don't let us yield to temptation,
10. but rescue us from the evil one.

Page 152: In the Know About H₂O

Across:
4. oceans
5. water
8. glaciers

Down:
1. boils
2. floats
3. ice
4. oxygen
6. gas
7. week

Page 153: Spot the Difference

Page 155: A Promise in the Sky

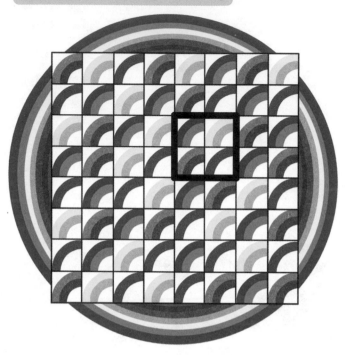

Page 156: A Graveyard of Ships

```
C S L A F A S L H Y O D Q A P
G H V L K C B Y D O U R Q S D
I I E U Q I Y X V N V I L N Y
R P D E P R L A E S H G L K K
A U I L T F E L E P H A N T S
F G Z O S A V O G X W B J C X
F U R N R L H H Q L X Z B G I
E A O A A C S V Z A U N C K T
C I R M V X S T H K G S Q S P
L L E B W E G W D C J D A Y E
I P F P E P Y O W A N O R Z V
L B W V B Z Z A F J C L V Q N
K R Y E A K C E R W P I H S Z
I N D E Z G H M Y D N P T C H
C J A G E Q N A M I B I A T X
```

Page 157: Go Ahead and Laugh

God will yet fill your mouth with **laughter**. And he will fill your lips with shouts of **joy**. —Job 8:21

A happy **heart** is like good **medicine**. —Proverbs 17:22

Then we were filled with **laughter**, and we sang **happy** songs. Then the other nations said, "The Lord has done **great** things for them." —Psalm 126:2

There is a time to **cry** and a time to **laugh**. —Ecclesiastes 3:4

"I have told you these things so that you can have the same **joy** I have. I want your **joy** to be the fullest **joy**." —John 15:11

"So you will go out with joy. You will be led out in peace. The **mountains** and hills will burst into song before you. All the **trees** in the fields will clap their hands." —Isaiah 55:12

Page 158: Follow That Nose!

Page 159: The Nose Knows

Across:	Down:
2. photograph	1. people
4. miles	3. smell
6. law	5. skin

Page 162: Coral Creations

Page 165: Around and Around and Around

MEET THE TEAM!

LOUiE GiGLiO is the pastor of Passion City Church and the original visionary of the Passion movement, which exists to call a generation to leverage their lives for the fame of Jesus. Since 1997, Passion has gathered collegiate-aged young people in events across the US and around the world, and it continues to see 18–25-year-olds fill venues across the nation. Most recently, Passion hosted over 700,000 people from over 150 countries online at Passion 2021. In addition to the Passion Conferences, Louie and his wife, Shelley, lead the teams at Passion City Church, sixstepsrecords, Passion Publishing, and the Passion Global Institute. Louie is the national bestselling author of *Don't Give the Enemy a Seat at Your Table*, *Not Forsaken*, *Goliath Must Fall*, *Indescribable*, *How Great Is Our God*, and *The Comeback*. Louie and Shelley make their home in Atlanta, Georgia, with their goldendoodle, London.

TAMA FORTNER is an ECPA award-winning and bestselling writer with more than forty titles to her credit. She has collaborated with some of the biggest names in Christian publishing to create inspirational books for both children and teens, as well as adults, including the wildly successful Indescribable Kids series and Jesus Calling for Kids series. But her greatest accomplishments happen in a happy little home on the outskirts of Nashville, Tennessee, where she lives with her family and an incredibly lazy dog, who doubles as a foot warmer.

NiCOLA ANDERSON has been an illustrator and graphic designer since she could hold a crayon in her hand but has been working professionally since 2001. After many years working in the design industry, she now crafts imaginary worlds from her home studio, AndoTwin Studio, in Manchester, UK. During this time, she has worked with an eclectic range of clients and has loved every minute!

LYNSEY WiLSON is an illustrator who works primarily in digital mediums. She uses a variety of contrasting styles, making her a highly versatile artist. She is passionately creative, from using inks and paper to working with fabrics to baking. Lynsey lives with her husband and two children and will often be found walking her beloved dog, Rufus, along the rain-swept forests, fields, and canals of North West England.

If you loved Pastor Louie's *Indescribable Activity Book for Kids,* then check out these other books in the Indescribable Kids series!

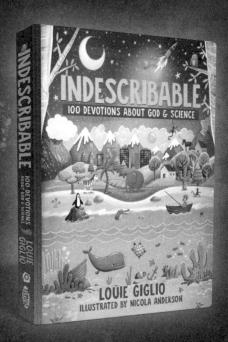

ISBN: 978-0-7180-8610-7
MSRP: $17.99

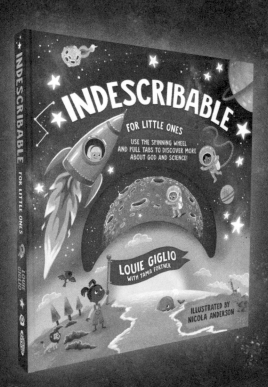

ISBN: 978-1-4002-2615-3
MSRP: $12.99

ISBN: 978-1-4002-1552-2
MSRP: $17.99

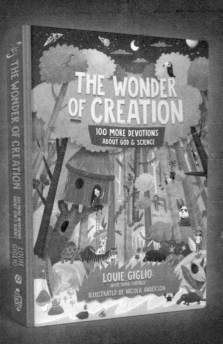

ISBN: 978-1-4002-3046-4
MSRP: $17.99

Visit IndescribableKids.com to learn more!

Written by Louie Giglio with Tama Fortner
Illustrated by Nicola Anderson and Lynsey Wilson
Images used under license from Shutterstock: sugar cookies © venski; pothos © Kristyna Vagnerova; marshmallow pattern © judyjump; marshmallow stack © Alfinna Damayanty; icing bag © AlyonaZhitnaya; cookie dough © Jakinnboaz; spoon © Olena Go; arctic ice © Tartila; spiral notebook © Marina Santiaga; pizza © Aleksangel

Printed in the USA

23 24 25 26 27 CWM 6 5 4 3 2 1

Mfr: CWM / Jefferson City, MO / April 2023 / PO #12167147